BRIGHT IDEAS

Inspirations for PHYSICAL EDUCATION

Published by Scholastic Ltd,
Villiers House,
Clarendon Avenue,
Leamington Spa,
Warwickshire CV32 5PR

© 1993 Scholastic Ltd
Revised edition 1995
3 4 5 6 7 8 9 6 7 8 9 0 1 2 3 4 5

Written by Carol Burton and
Graeme Kent
Edited by Juliet Gladston
Sub-edited by Catherine Bywater
Designed by Sue Limb
Series designed by Juanita Puddifoot
Illustrated by Ian Heard
Cover design by Sue Limb
Cover artwork by Nancy Anderson

Designed using Aldus Pagemaker
Processed by Pages Bureau,
Leamington Spa
Artwork by David Harban Design,
Warwick
Printed in Great Britain by
Ebenezer Baylis & Son, Worcester

**British Library Cataloguing in
Publication Data**
A catalogue record for this book is
available from the British Library.

ISBN 0-590-53517-X 2nd revised edition
(ISBN 0-590-53049-6 1st edition)

CONTENTS

INTRODUCTION

Physical education

In theory, physical education should be one of the easier areas of the curriculum to teach in the primary school. Most children actively enjoy the subject and are eager to respond to it in a positive manner. They usually welcome the chance to get out of the classroom and into the hall or playground. If they are not pushed too hard or too quickly, they love having the opportunity to control their bodies and stretch their minds while developing fresh skills and mastering different types of apparatus.

Yet, despite the fact that PE is 'pre-sold' to most young children, it has to be said that often the subject is approached with considerable apprehension and trepidation by primary school teachers, especially since the introduction of the National Curriculum. Many feel that it is a highly technical subject and thus unsuitable for the non-specialist, who may not have sufficient knowledge or experience of the different strands which make up the modern PE programme. There is also an erroneous impression that in order to teach PE successfully it is necessary for the teacher to be possessed of considerable sporting ability.

It is certainly a fact that the majority of primary teachers are not PE specialists. In a survey carried out by the Central Council of Physical Education in 1992 it was discovered that while 89 per cent of primary teachers taught PE, fewer than 10 per cent had any formal qualifications or coaching certificates in the subject. Nevertheless, it is perfectly possible for all teachers to share in and capitalise upon their pupil's enthusiasm for movement in order to make PE a vital and integral part of the curriculum.

BACKGROUND

This book has been written to help anyone involved in teaching PE, but in particular the non-specialist. It incorporates many aspects of good teaching practice with modern research findings and the needs of the National Curriculum at Key Stages 1 and 2. The activities are essentially practical, designed to help the busy teacher who has little time to organise the mass of material available. It provides a progressively-designed series of practical and appropriate activities for children at different stages of their growth. All the ideas have been used over a number of years in the writers' own schools with children of all ages, from reception to first year secondary.

Successful physical education

A successful physical education programme should involve all children and the whole child. It should provide an essential all-round grounding for the child, physically, mentally, emotionally and socially.

A carefully-prepared programme will also develop the health, fitness and co-ordination of the children, helping them to regard exercise as natural and enjoyable, thus laying the foundation for later life.

The activities of such a programme will assist children in coping with success and failure, help their self-esteem and develop habits of good living. They will be given practice in co-operation, mutual trust, team-work, tolerance and forming good relationships. The mental skills involved – of problem-solving, decision-making, planning, observing and assessing – will stand them in good stead in many other areas of their lives, both in and out of school.

How to use this book

The book has been divided into a number of chapters, one for each of the component parts of the National Curriculum:
• athletics;
• dance;
• games;
• gymnastic activities;
• outdoor and adventurous activities;
• swimming.

Each of these chapters is broken down into a number of practical activities, which are designed for various ages in the primary school. These activities can be used in a number of ways. If you have already planned the PE curriculum in your school then they may be used as resource material, to be dipped into and used as and when required. Although the activities have been aimed at specific age groups, most of them can be adapted and used quite easily to suit all ages. However, if you have not planned the PE curriculum in your school the activities can be used as the basis for developing a programme. This way you can work through them as a progressive scheme. The National Curriculum requirements for the whole school may be set by judicious selection of the activities presented here. Suggestions as to how this may be achieved are given in Chapter 7.

When working with children during PE lessons make sure that the lessons consist of a mixture of directed activity and of children discovering for themselves. Constant and progressive practice is an essential ingredient of the programme. The emphasis should always be on performing rather than discussing.

Children will achieve a progression in their performance of a skill or action by evaluating it at each stage and by judging the work of their peers. The pattern to be followed here is plan/perform/evaluate.

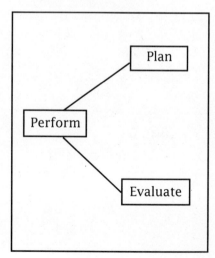

CHAPTER 1

Athletic activities

The requirements of the National Curriculum are simple. At Key Stage 2 the children are encouraged to run, jump and throw with accuracy, speed, height, length and distance. The children should be given the chance to measure, compare and improve their performance.

The programmes of study in this chapter are intended to allow children to fulfil these requirements and should be viewed across the key stage and not year by year.

Many of the skills required by the programmes of study will be developed in other areas of activity, for example, throwing in games and jumping in gymnastics and dance. Make sure that you begin each session with a suitable warm-up and finish with a period of cool-down in which the children gently reduce their level of activity before returning to the classroom. This part of the session could be planned by the children as they progress.

There are many integral skills in athletic performances and the amount which can be taught will depend upon the age of the children. However, there are skills which are appropriate for every age. The secret is to build up the level of skills slowly, starting with very simple concepts which will form the basis of the more complex skills required at a later stage. As a rough guide the following suggestions show the skills which average age groups should hope to achieve. However, they may be adapted to the needs of the children.

• Year 3 (seven to eight): running, relays and sprints, throwing and long jump, different forms of travelling including walking and skipping.
• Year 4 (eight to nine): sprinting, walking, throwing and jumping.
• Year 5 (nine to ten): sprinting, longer distance running, throwing and jumping.
• Year 6 (ten to eleven): sprinting, longer distance running, throwing, jumping and more competitive events.

ACTIVITIES

1. Running with an object and passing it

Age range
Seven to eight.

Group size
Individuals, pairs and groups of four.

What you need
Cones, chalk, hoops, skittles, small rubber balls, plastic bats, quoits, small sticks.

What to do
Use the games in this activity as the basis for a number of moving and passing activities which can extend over a number of weeks.

Begin the session by letting the children play a warm-up game of tag. After this, mark out the distance of 10m with cones or chalk and organise the children into pairs. Give each pair a rubber ball and ask one child in each pair to run to the end of the 10m line, carrying the ball, and run back again. She must then pass the ball to her partner, who should repeat the performance.

Remind the children that they must not start running until the ball is in their hands. Observe them carefully and point out any faults they may have with their running actions.

Let the children run about the area by themselves and tell them that when you shout you want them to move their arms twice as fast as their legs. After a couple of minutes, tell the children to slow down again until they are jogging normally. Then tell them to run so that their arms are moving at half the speed of their legs. After a while, stop them and ask what they felt happened to their running speed when their arms moved quicker and when they moved slower than their legs.

Tell the children that their legs will move quickly without them having to think too much, if they concentrate on their arm movements.

Ask the children to reform into their pairs. Tell them that they are going to race their partners. Stress the need for speed and remind them that they should concentrate on their arm actions if they want to run quickly. Allow the children to race one another several times, then repeat the ball-relay activity a number of times, with the partners running and passing the ball to one another.

Next, ask each pair to join another pair to make groups of four. Organise more activities which involve running and passing the ball, emphasising the need for speed. When the children have grasped the principle of one child running at a time and then passing a ball, divide each team so that two children stand at the far end of the line and tell them to run from end to end, passing the ball. (The first child runs to the second, who runs back to the third and so on.)

Once the children have grasped this concept they can progress to moving in different ways as they pass the

10 m

ball from one end of the line to the other, for example, hopping, skipping and jumping.

Introduce plastic bats to the game. The children should work in pairs and they can walk, run and finally hop while balancing a ball or bean bag on their bat as they move towards their partners. If they drop the ball they must stop, pick it up and put it back on the bat.

Organise another relay. Using teams of four, arrange the children so that they are standing at the same end of the course. At the far end place a large hoop, with four small balls inside it. The first child in each team should also hold a ball. On the command 'go', the first child must run, holding the ball, to the hoop, pick up another ball and run back to the second child. He must then pass one ball to the second child and retain the other. The second child, in turn, must run to the hoop, holding the ball, pick up another ball, run back to the third child, hand over one ball and so on. At the end of the race each child in the team should be holding a ball.

Repeat this race, but this time put other objects inside the hoops – quoits, small sticks and so on. From time to time change the method of travelling from running to skipping, hopping or walking.

Once the children have mastered the idea of the relay running the possibilities are endless – skipping, sack races and so on.

2. Relays and running in lanes

Age range
Eight to nine.

Group size
Individuals, pairs and groups of four.

What you need
A marked running track, balls, hoops, sacks, ropes, eggs and spoons, bats, bean bags, skipping ropes.

What to do
Use the following exercises as the basis for a number of sessions involving movement and team work. Running in lanes is not an easy concept for infants to grasp and this activity may take some time to teach and learn.

Let the children warm-up with a short period of free running and then show the children the marked lanes (if you don't have a marked track use long ropes to mark off the lanes). Explain that when a race is run each person in the race must keep within their lane so as not to get in the way of the other runners.

Having explained to the children how a track is used, they can start to run races over short distances. Limit the number of children involved in each race to about three or four to begin with. Once you know their abilities, always have children of roughly similar speeds competing with one another. You should also begin to impress on them that

they should run *over* the finishing line rather than simply up to it.

When you are satisfied that the children have grasped the concept of running in lanes introduce the idea of relay races. They can start off in pairs and fours, running from one end of the track to the other and passing a small ball. The children can also try walking, hopping and skipping, as well as running.

Follow on from this simple lane practice by allowing the children time to skip with a rope. Afterwards, move on to demonstrate how to jump inside a sack. You can then organise relay races in which the children must skip with ropes and then jump in sacks.

Allow the children more time on their own in which to develop their skipping techniques, stopping them to allow good practitioners to demonstrate ideas and techniques. Encourage them to expand their repertoire by trying to skip backwards, turning the rope twice with each jump or using different jumps.

As the children become more confident with a variety of techniques and movements introduce them to other forms of relay racing. For example, they could balance bean bags on their heads or begin to practise egg-and-spoon races.

Walking provides good co-ordination practice for young children. Ask them to show you their fastest walk. Pick out one or two examples of good practice and ask these children to perform in front of the others while you emphasise the good points of their walking techniques. Stress that when walking quickly they should be almost, but not quite, running. However, both feet – the heel of one foot and the toe of the other foot – should always be in contact with the floor at the same time.

End the session with a series of walking relay races.

3. Obstacle races

Age range
Eight to nine.

Group size
Individuals, pairs and groups of four.

What you need
Bean bags, plastic bats, skittles, ropes, hoops, balls.

What to do
Use obstacle races as the basis for a number of sessions, coaching and developing the individual skills needed to complete the courses as they become more exacting.

Let the children warm-up by playing a game of tag. Then explain the principle of the obstacle race to the children and ask them to suggest obstacles which could be used in a race of this kind.

With the aid of the children, lay out an obstacle course. Try to arrange it so that the

participants will have a chance to use the athletic skills which they have learned previously, such as running in lanes, skipping and so on. An example of such a race may be:
• begin on a start line and carry a bean bag on a plastic bat;
• reach a cane which has been placed across two skittles;
• put down the bean bag and bat and go under the cane;
• collect a football and dribble round some markers;
• leave the football and bowl a hoop to another marker;
• put down the hoop and run to the finish line.

Before starting the obstacle race, go through all the movements which will be required. Then give the children some time in which they can practise by themselves the various skills involved – balancing, dribbling a football, bowling a hoop and so on.

Let the children run over the course several times before you start the race so that they can familiarise themselves

with the conditions. It may alsobe useful to appoint teams of 'monitors' from some of the children who are not running in a particular race to help you replace the equipment.

Finally, you can run a series of obstacle races, first with individual children running against one another and then organising relay races with teams of two and then four competing. In the relay races each runner must run back to the starting line and touch the next competitor before he begins to run.

The monitors will have to move quickly to replace the obstacles, so they will need to be waiting along the side of the track as the race takes place.

With the aid of the children, develop as many different types of obstacle races as you can, utilising all the equipment available in the school. Bearing

in mind safety considerations, it may also be possible to include natural obstacles such as trees.

A number of these obstacle races should also involve the children jumping as well as running and skipping. Take time to teach and demonstrate the standing long jump. To do this jump the child must stand on a line with a thick mat in front of her. Emphasise that, as in running, the correct use of the arms is very important. The child should stand in a semi-crouched position, with both arms extended behind her. Then as she jumps she should sweep both arms forward, leaping as high as possible – bending her knees as she lands to absorb the impact.

Spend a number of sessions on the triple jump and long jump, keeping records of the distances reached by the children and marking their improvement in technique and confidence.

4. Jumping

Age range
Nine to ten.

Group size
Individuals and pairs.

What you need
Tape-measure, sand-pit (if available), mats, skipping ropes.

What to do
Let the children warm-up with a period of free skipping with ropes. Then revise the principles of the standing long jump (see Activity 3) and move on to teach and demonstrate the standing triple jump. To accomplish a standing triple jump the children will have to put together a hop, a step and a jump. (Remember to emphasise the importance of landing correctly.)

Start by teaching the hop. Line the children up and ask them to try and put the three parts of the sequence together. If there is a sand-pit available use it, otherwise place mats ready for the children to jump on to.

When the children have had plenty of time to practise the sequence, remind them of the importance of the arm action when jumping. Ask them to concentrate on swinging their arms forward whenever they feel this will help them to gain distance.

Towards the end of the session, begin to measure some of the jumps, so that the children will have standards to aim at.

End the session by revising the principles of the standing long jump and allowing the children to practise this. Then introduce a run-up to their long jumps. Encourage the children to take off from each foot at first, so that they get to know which is their stronger foot. They can practise by taking three steps before they jump, taking off with one foot in a big hopping action, but aiming to land on two feet. Let them do this for some time, then allow the children to practise the long jump with a run-up in their own way.

5. Throwing

Age range
Nine to ten.

Group size
Individuals and pairs.

What you need
Rounders balls, cricket balls, tape-measure, soft balls.

What to do
Let the children warm-up by throwing soft balls, running after them and retrieving them. You should then demonstrate the technique of the standing throw. Stress to the children that they are only allowed to retrieve their balls when they are told to do so. This avoids children running in front of others who may still be throwing. (This activity may be linked with those on throwing in Chapter 3.)

When the children begin to throw, stand them in a line. Usually, boys throw cricket balls and girls throw rounders balls, but this really depends upon the strength and size of each individual child, so do not be dogmatic about this. Tell the child to hold the ball in her hand so that her palm faces upwards. She should move her hand so that the ball is near to her ear – on her throwing side – and her weight is back. Make sure that she stands sideways to the direction she will be throwing and that her throwing arm is furthest away from where she will throw. Tell the child to take her weight back and at the same time take her throwing arm back. She should then bring her weight and bent throwing arm forward. She should release the ball upwards and point her throwing hand upwards, bringing it down to the opposite knee.

Allow the children plenty of time to practise throwing their balls and when they seem to have grasped the technique move on to practise the running throw. Start by asking the children to run three paces before they release the ball, and then let them gradually increase this to five, seven, nine and finally eleven paces. The release action used for a running throw is the same as that for a standing throw. In fact the children will actually be stationary when the ball is released – the run-up is merely to give the throw added impetus.

Watch the children practise the running throw and check that their movements are smooth and fluid. Make sure that they do not develop the habit of running, stopping dead and then beginning the throwing action. Encourage them to make the sequence much more flowing, with only the briefest of stops before the ball is released.

Spend a number of sessions working on throws, using games and competitions to add interest and variety to the training sessions.

6. Sprint starting

Age range
Ten to eleven.

Group sizes
Individuals.

What you need
Marked running track or ropes and chalk.

What to do
Let the children warm-up by allowing them to run around the area, but stopping and running on the spot at the command from you. Then move on to demonstrate and teach the sprint start.

Tell the children to line up behind a marked line and teach them the following procedure:
• 'On your marks' – kneel on one knee and put both hands behind the line. Extend the thumbs and fingers of both hands to make bridges. Stare about three metres ahead at the track. Adjust the overall position until it is a comfortable one.
• 'Get set' – raise the hips and bring the body weight so that it is over the shoulders. Keep the arms straight so that the position is such that it would be impossible to take the hands away without falling over. Keep very still.
• 'Go' – push off on the back foot. Keep low at first driving legs and arms as hard as possible.

Allow the children to practise each stage of the sprint start, correcting their techniques where necessary.

Gradually allow them to put the three stages together into a whole movement and then allow some time for them to practise the complete start sequence.

Supervise the children as they use the sprint start over ever-increasing distances, first over 10m, then 15m, 20m and so on, up to a full 100m race.

Use the sprint start for all races in future sessions. Most children of this age will not have the skill or strength to perfect the movement, but they will have grasped the basic technique before they leave primary school.

7. Passing the baton

Age range
Ten to eleven.

Group size
Pairs and groups.

What you need
Batons, a circular running track (optional).

What to do
Warm-up by organising a game of chain tag in which two children work together to catch a third child. When the third child is caught he links up with the other two, as does the next child tagged and so on.

Once the children are properly warmed-up teach and demonstrate two basic methods of passing the baton in a relay race.

The two main methods are:
• *the up-sweep pass*: where the baton is placed firmly and decisively in the receiver's hand with an upward movement of the arm;
• *the down-sweep pass*: where the baton is placed firmly in the receiver's palm with a downward movement of the arm.

Organise the children into pairs to practise passing the baton, first using the up-sweep pass and then the down-sweep pass. To begin with this should be carried out at a walking pace. One child must wait, looking back towards the second child who walks towards him slowly and places the baton in his outstretched arm (neither child must slap or snatch). The child receiving

the baton should already be moving slowly when he receives the baton. The speed at which the children move can be gradually increased as they become more skilled at passing the baton.

Allow the children to keep practising these movements at walking pace and slow running pace, until the techniques have been grasped. Thereafter, move to the circular track and place the children into teams of four. You can then hold a series of races between the teams, using either the up-sweep or down-sweep passes. Ask each team to decide in advance which form of pass they are going to use – they can experiment with the other type in a later race.

Allow the children plenty of space in which to make the change-overs and give them plenty of opportunities to run and pass the baton.

8. Cross country

Age range
Nine to eleven.

Group size
Individuals.

What you need
Stop-watch, bench, skipping rope, circular running track.

What to do
Preparation for cross country running could occupy as many as five or six weeks. Therefore,

this activity has been set out on a week by week basis to show the necessary preparation.

Start each session with general warm-up activities, starting at the top of the body and working downward with various stretching exercises.

• Neck: ask the children to move their heads from side to side, trying to get their ears to touch their shoulders. Repeat this three times each side.

• Shoulders: ask the children to make small circular movements with both shoulders moving at the same time.

• Arms: ask the children to stretch both arms out to their sides and then wiggle their fingers and rotate their wrists and elbows in both directions. Tell them to extend their arms straight above their heads and push upwards with both arms in turn. Ask them to keep their arms above their heads and then bring them down to shoulder level, still extended outwards, and gently push back against the shoulder joint. They should repeat this three times.

• Waist: tell the children to place their hands on their hips and slowly stretch one arm in the air so that it touches the ear on that side of their bodies. They should then push upwards in a diagonal direction over their heads, stretching their waists in the process. There should be no forwards movement. They should repeat this three times on each side.

• Legs: ask the children to stand on one leg, with their hands on their hips to aid balance. They should lift one leg, bend it at the knee and rotate the ankle, knee and hip forwards and backwards five times each way. Tell them to repeat this with the other leg. They should then stand with their legs together and cross one leg over the other. Keeping their knees slightly bent, ask them to curl gently downwards and try to touch the floor with their finger. They should go down as far as possible without strain. They should repeat this three times then cross over the other leg.

Ask the children to stand with their legs apart and lean over one leg so that the other is extended sideways. The children must keep their backs straight as they extend. Tell them to repeat this three times (coming back to the start position and then leaning again counts as one repetition) and then repeat this movement using their other leg.

Having warmed-up properly you should take the children through one of the weekly training programmes, working progressively from week one.

Week one
Go on a class run of approximately 800m, according to the abilities of the children. Try to get further adult help in timing the children as they finish. Use this time as the criterion for improvement.

Week two

Progress to making interval runs. The children should sprint 20m and then walk back to where they started from. Ask them to repeat three times. If you use a netball court or something similar you can structure the distances so that they run progressively further each time, starting with the first line. Let the children rest between runs and repeat this three times.

Use the netball court or other marked area and let the children run around the straight lines at a jogging pace and then sprint across the diagonals.

Week three

Bring out a bench and a skipping rope and place them against a wall. Ask the children to perform step-ups on to the bench by placing one foot and then the other on to the bench and then placing one foot and then the other back on to the ground. Let the children do this for one minute, rest and then do it for another minute.

Next, the children can practise doing sit-ups. They should work in pairs so that one child lies on the floor, with her knees bent upwards and with her arms crossed over her chest while her partner holds her feet down and counts how many sit-ups are performed in a minute. A sit-up consists of the child bringing her elbows forward from a lying position so that they touch her thighs as she sits up with her arms crossed over her chest. Make sure that the children exchange positions.

Allow the children to skip for a minute, rest for a minute and then skip for a further minute. Finally, move the children against a wall so that they stand sideways against it. Tell them to touch the floor, bending their knees, and then leap up to touch as high a spot on the wall as they can reach. Encourage them to do this for a minute and then rest for a minute and then carry on for another minute.

Week four

Repeat the activities from Week two, but ask the children to perform five interval runs instead of three.

Week five

Go with the children on a class run over country for about 800m or any other distance considered within the capabilities of the children. The timing is not important, but make it a competitive run, giving points for each placing, from first to last.

Week six

Give the children another 800m run, but time them on this occasion and compare their times with those from Week one. Present certificates or something similar to all those children who have improved upon their first times (see photocopiable page 190).

CHAPTER 2

Dance

The purposes of dance at Key Stage 1 are:
• to develop control, co-ordination, balance, poise and elevation in the basic actions of travelling, jumping, turning, gesture and stillness;
• to perform movements or patterns, including some from existing dance traditions;
• to explore moods and feelings and to develop their response to music through dances, by using rhythmic responses and contrasts of speed, shape, direction and level.

At Key Stage 2, children should be guided to:
• enrich their movements;
• increase the range and complexity of their body actions;
• to develop more complex dances, as well as expressing feelings and creating simple characters and narrative movement.

The purpose of this chapter is to help teachers approach these aims by providing dances and dance ideas. These ideas for dance can come from work being covered in most areas of the curriculum.

BACKGROUND

When introducing dance, start by using stimuli which the children are likely to be familiar with. At this stage fun and play should be important components of any dance activities. Repetition and whole body movements are also very important and the children's movements should be action-packed. This will enable them to explore how and what their bodies can do as well as develop control over their bodies and movements.

When the children are more confident and experienced in dance they should be encouraged to broaden their vocabulary of movement. Ingredients such as fine touch, lingering, sustained and robust movement should all enter the repertoire of primary school children before the end of Key Stage 2.

During the first years of teaching dance it will be advisable to concentrate on solo or small group work to avoid children hiding in large groups. Younger children in particular may find the whole concept of organised dance a little overwhelming at first. The class may certainly dance together as a communal activity but, at least in the initial stages, such whole-class activities would be better consisting of each child performing her individual dance within the overall class movement.

At Key Stage 1 try to keep dance ideas fairly simple, but repetitive with short phrases of movement, as younger children have limited attention and memory spans. Emphasise that at all times their starting and finishing positions are important.

The children may work individually and in pairs (mirroring, copying, following and so on), or in small groups (the same movements used in pairs, plus circles, lines and so on).

Music and sound are not always necessary, but if they are employed they can be used in a variety of ways. For example, they can provide a rhythm for the children to dance to, an accompaniment, or can be used to create atmosphere. The children could also make up their own sounds for dancing, which could be followed up later on in a music session.

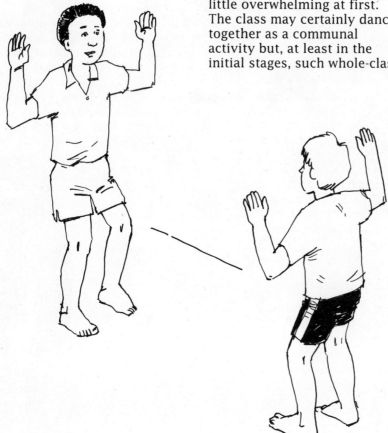

ACTIVITIES

Dances

1. Fireworks

Age range
Four to five.

Group size
Individuals and small groups.

What you need
Pictures, chanting poems such as 'Remember, remember the fifth of November', tambour, music such as *Oxygene IV* by Jean Michel Jarre (optional).

What to do
Let the children warm-up by walking to the beat of a tambour. Tell them to walk and stop to a count of eight. Repeat this but tell the children that this time, on 'eight', they should turn and walk in a different direction.

As this will probably be one of the first dances the children have performed they will need plenty of instruction to begin with. Organise them into groups of three or four and allocate each group a separate part of the room or hall. (These groups will begin work later in the session, after the children have completed the individual activities.)

Ask the children to think of the names and functions of different fireworks such as rockets, Catherine wheels, sparklers and so on. As you discuss these fireworks it may be a good idea to stress the safety aspects and the Firework Code. Tell the children to choose three types of firework and demonstrate what they do. For example, for rockets the children could stand straight up, with their arms by their sides making a rocket shape. They can then 'explode' by jumping in the air and making a star shape. Work on these together, developing and refining movements.

Ask the children what happens to a firework after it has been let off. They can then work this into the ending of their sequence so that on landing – remembering to bend their knees to absorb impact – they can sink slowly to the floor and lie perfectly still. They should then count to five in their heads and rise to a standing position, spreading their arms out to their sides and keeping their knees slightly bent, and do the actions of another firework.

For example, they can twirl round like a Catherine wheel, doing three turns and sinking slowly to the ground.

The children should now move into their groups of four, and work on the combined part of the dance. Tell them to form a line in their groups and number each child from one to four. Tell them to keep still for a count of five. Then the first child in the group should jump upwards, keeping a straight shape. The other children in the group then follow fairly rapidly, but maintaining a gap between each leap, to give a 'Mexican wave effect'. As the children land they 'die' and keep very still.

Next, still working in groups, the children should rehearse the whole dance, from individual movements to group efforts. You may want to play some music to accompany them and they can add sounds too if they like.

Ask the groups to keep practising and rehearsing until they are ready to demonstrate their whole dances, working either as a complete class or in their groups.

2. Bubbles

Age range
Five to six.

Group size
Individuals.

What you need
Bubble blowing kit (balloons could be substituted here), music such as *Gymnopédies* by Erik Satie (optional).

What to do
Let the children blow bubbles. Ask them to try and avoid bursting them if they can. What words can they use to describe the movements of the bubbles?

Now ask the children to try and copy the bubbles' movements. They should try to be light and airy, wobbly and shakey. They can also roll like a bubble around the room.

Tell the children to imagine that they are inside a bubble. They should gently explore their surroundings remembering that if they push too hard the bubble will burst. Can they move with the bubble around the room? How does it move (rolling, bouncing)? Don't forget to remind the children to work at different levels, direction and speed. Do the children enjoy being in the bubble?

Suddenly, tell the children that their bubbles have burst. How do they feel? What do they do?

Tell the children to pretend that they are in another bubble, but this one is made of sticky toffee. How will the movements be different?

Finally, ask the children to combine the soapy bubble movements with the sticky bubble movements, using a linking movement between the two.

3. Playground games

Age range
Six to seven.

Group size
Individuals, pairs and small groups.

What you need
A whistle or tambour, music such as 'Filleted Place' by The Shadows (optional).

What to do
Ask the children to warm-up by running round in a big circle. Make sure that they are all running in the same direction. When you blow the whistle they must stop, turn 90° and run round again. Repeat this several times.

Once the children have warmed-up ask them to talk about the games that are played in the playground, for example:
• line walking (if patterns have been painted on the playground);
• hopscotch;
• skipping;
• French skipping;
• patacake;
• tiggy;
• marbles;
• football;
• clapping sequences.

Ask the children to choose three or four games and imitate their movements; for example jumping from one foot to two feet to one foot like in hopscotch. Ask the children to include a balance or a moment of stillness and remind them to think about their body shapes as they do this. Having completed the balance they can continue the movement they were doing before.

Ask the children to join with a partner and teach each other their sequences. They can do this by working side by side or as a form of follow-the-leader. Once they have learned both dances they can put the two together so that one is performed after the other.

Ask the children to work in pairs again and develop a step pattern along an imaginary line. They will need to decide whether the line is straight, angular or wiggly. Timing is essential here but they can choose whenever to copy or follow-the-leader.

Finally, they can finish their dances by having a clap sequence with a chant if they want to.

Encourage the children to repeat their whole dance through twice, so that each part of the dance is identical the second time around.

4. Machines

Age range
Seven to eight.

Group size
Individuals, small groups or the whole class.

What you need
Music such as 'Welcome to the Machine' from *Wish You Were Here* by Pink Floyd, or *The Sorcerer's Apprentice* by Dukas (optional). You may wish to bring some machines into the hall, maybe look at the inside of a watch.

What to do
Ask the children to walk round the hall in straight, direct lines going to every corner. Tell them to stop suddenly and make sharp turns on their way.

Take everyday actions and ask the children to make them machine-like by adding lots of 'freeze-frames'. For example, cleaning teeth, stacking boxes from the floor to a shelf, or even simply walking! Tell them to imagine that someone is taking lots of pictures of them as they move and at every click of the camera they should freeze, as if captured in a photograph. This process will make their movements

become stilted and robotic. If the same movements are repeated over and over again the whole thing becomes mechanical.

Ask the children to walk, stop suddenly and hold their shape as if in a 'freeze-frame'. They should then do a sudden turn, using their whole bodies, and bend down to pick up an imaginary box. This whole process should include lots of 'freeze-frames'. They can then pretend to put the box on to a shelf.

Once the children have rehearsed this movement individually, they can work in pairs and teach each other their movements. Let them rehearse in their pairs and try to link their movements together, remembering to keep them staccato the whole time. Having done this, the children can join with another pair and add their movements together. They should keep joining in this way until the whole class is involved.

The children might also like to explore the idea of a machine getting out of control, speeding up, exploding, wearing out and slowly 'dying'.

Further activity
The dance idea of machines could be extended to make a whole class machine, rather like the inside of a watch, where one child's or group of children's movement initiates the next child's/group of children's movement and so on.

5. Toys

Age range
Eight to nine.

Group size
Individuals, small groups and the whole class.

What you need
Drums, music such as *Golliwogs Cakewalk* by Debussy, 'Air' by Tomita from *Snowflakes are Dancing* or any marching music.

What to do
Let the children warm-up by exploring their own ideas of marching. Are they carrying a gun? Do they salute? Encourage them to do high kicking steps or high knee lifts. They could also try

varying the speeds and direction of their marches. How does a soldier change direction?

Tell the children to imagine that they are toy soldiers who have come to life for a night. They should pretend to be lined up on a shelf in a toy shop. In pairs, the children should explore the toy shop, but they have to come down from the shelf first! As they explore the children should march in step. Timing is essential, so they will need to spend some time on perfecting their joint march.

Once the children have had time to explore, including how they turn and join up with each other, they can join up with another pair to make four and teach each other their movements. They can then join up to make eight, until finally the whole class is working together.

Further activity
The children can explore moving like dolls, teddy bears, trains and so on. Perhaps the whole class could do a dance which involves different groups of children being different toys?

6. The creeps!

Age range
Nine to ten.

Group size
Individuals and small groups.

What you need
Music such as *The Pink Panther Theme* by Mancini (optional).

What to do
Tell the children to close their eyes and, by moving their hands out in front of them, feel their way around the hall. If they touch any one or anything they must change direction. They must not talk or make any sounds as they do this.

Having warmed-up, you can now set the scene. Tell the children that it is the middle

of the night and they are alone in an old house. They can see very little in front of them, there may be stairs or steep drops and there are cobwebs everywhere. Tell them that they are very frightened.

The children must then explore the house, walking around very cautiously, brushing away cobwebs, testing stairs, stopping and starting and so on. They should work at a fairly low height and feel their way as they did in the warm-up.

Now put on the music and let the children try their walk to the music for a couple of minutes. Also introduce the idea that they may be being followed. They should keep looking behind to check.

Tell the children to join up with a partner and work in pairs. They should walk towards each other from opposite directions, doing their own walk until they meet. Is this a friend or an enemy? The children should circle each other, sizing each other up until they decide whether their partner is a friend or foe. If a friend they should make friendly gestures, or if an enemy they can have a mock fight. Emphasise that the 'fight' should be a non-contact one and it can end by one partner sinking to the ground and the other retreating.

Can the children now fit the sequence of movements with the music? They may need some guidance here. Remind them that phrases of their dance can be repeated.

7. The circus:1

Age range
Ten to eleven.

Group size
Individuals and small groups.

What you need
Mats, whistle, music such as marches by Sousa, 'The Entertainer' by Joplin or the 'Comedian's Gallop' by Rimsky-Korsakof (optional).

What to do
Let the children warm-up by walking round the area and pretending to juggle. They should watch their balls making sure they do not collide with each other. Blow the whistle and tell the children to move like prancing horses. Blow the whistle again and tell the children to pretend to be clowns – waving, smiling, crying, laughing and so on.

The following dance is based on a circus theme. The children will need to explore the ideas in some detail, while bearing in mind such concepts as pathways, shape, level, speed, step, patterns and tension.

The dance itself may be broken up into sections which can be explored over several weeks and then drawn together to form a dance which has a definite beginning, middle and end. The children

will also need to be given plenty of time to practise and refine the content of each section and then the whole dance.

The following is an example of how such a dance may be composed using clowns as the main theme. The children may, however, decide to explore different acts. Tell the class to think of as many circus acts as they can. They should be persuaded to select any three of these acts and then to work on each in separate lessons. If, for example, the children choose clowns as one of their three subjects, this could be the topic of the first lesson.

Tell the children to work individually on their funny walks and pieces of comedy. Pick out good examples of each to be demonstrated to the rest of the class. Alternatively, pick out a Charlie Chaplin type walk to get the children started. Ask them to practise this, walking with their feet turned out, with slightly bent knees, and one arm twirling an imaginary cane. Proceed from this to the children's own walks.

Next, introduce the idea of rhythm such as 'slow, slow, quick, quick, slow'. The

children can then walk to the edge of a mat, where they can perform a 'trip'. This could lead into a forward roll or into a small jump, in which their feet are thrown forwards and they land on their bottoms, using their hands to take some of the impact.

The children can then stand and start to run and jump, with a pedalling motion in mid-air. Finally, they should land on both feet, bending their knees to absorb the impact of the landing, and take a deep bow.

This activity will form the first section of the dance and the beginning of the next. Allow the children time to perfect and refine this opening section for the rest of the session before moving on to the following activity.

8. The circus: 2

Age range
Ten to eleven.

Group size
Individuals.

What you need
Music (as in the previous activity).

What to do
Repeat the warm-up from the previous activity and then revise the work which the children did in Activity 2. The deep bow. This can be used as a linking movement between sections and from this the children will need to move on to select another circus act. If, for example, they choose tightrope walking they might work in the following way.

Tell them to stand up straight with their arms extended on either side, as if balancing on a rope. Ask them to consider the ways in which a tightrope walker might move along the rope. The general movement consists of the feet being turned out and placed one in front of another along a straight pathway. Demonstrate this to the children and tell them that they must use their arms to show that they are constantly battling for balance and that their bodies must reflect the tension of the movements.

Next, tell the children to introduce rhythm, for example, 'one step, two steps, big wobble'. The children should retain their balance and assume the original tightrope movement and then run to an imaginary platform at the end of the rope. They should then turn 180° and take a deep bow. Again, the bow marks the end of this section of the dance.

Give the class time to practise and refine this second section of their dances. Use suitable taped music to accompany them if you wish.

Having practised this second section, either with or without music, the children can combine the two sections

they have worked on so far, and work on this for the rest of the session.

9. The circus: 3

Age range
Ten to eleven.

Group size
Individuals and small groups.

What you need
Mats, music (as in Activity 7).

What to do
Use the same warm-up as in Activity 7. Then revise the work done in the previous two activities before progressing to the final section of their dance.

The class may decide to introduce a number of animal acts into their dance. If so, allow time to talk about the animals they wish to emulate. They could then move into small groups, with each group portraying the same animal.

The children should devise 'typical' movements for the animals they are going to portray. Elephants, for example, could walk round in a circle, linking trunks and tails and making strong, slow actions. Tigers and lions might use their front paws in clawing actions, walking in a slow, light-footed, but menacing manner. If the children do decide to portray lions and tigers child could be the animal trainer.

Impress upon the children, as they work in their groups, that they should keep their animal movements simple, because they are working on an overall impression. If their actions are too complicated the overall impression will lose its impact.

When the children have decided upon their group movements ask them to adapt these to a circular pathway. Encourage them to bring this section to a climax by each group adopting a pattern so that three children are in front and one behind. If there is another child in the group she should stand at the back, thus making a triangular pattern.

Still keeping to their animal movements as far as possible, the three children in the front of each group should kneel down on all fours. The two children behind them should step forward and climb on to their backs, making sure that they use their hips and shoulders to support the children. If there is still one child left in the group she should walk to the front of the balancing children and raise her arms as the signal for the children on top to climb down and stand back one pace. The supporters must adopt a kneeling position and the whole group can take a final bow to signify the end of the dance.

Complete the session by allowing the children to practise this section and, if time permits, join it to the two sections already rehearsed.

Over the next two or three sessions rehearse and refine the complete dance and then let the children demonstrate it, with or without music, either in groups or as a class.

Dance ideas

Almost any ideas may be used to spark off dance activities. Fantasy objects like robots or spacemen are popular as they provide a whole range of possible movements. Seasons of the year and aspects of weather are also often used as the basis for a dance activity. Poems, pieces of literature, pictures, pieces of music are all useful, while the children themselves are usually full of ideas.

As the children progress and grow more confident you will be able to use abstract ideas with them. A dance based on the idea of pathways, for example, could be used to bring in concepts such as direction, speed and tension.

The following ideas are intended to be used as starting points for dance. Each idea can be explored in one session or built up over a number of weeks. If you are not confident about teaching dance then start off by using concrete ideas – those based in reality – so that you know what sort of movements to expect. Later on you can move on to look at more abstract themes.

In all these ideas the aim is to use the imitation as a stepping stone towards dance; where the feelings and emotions, the pathways and movements are taken from the imitation and explored and exaggerated so becoming dance. There are many areas of dance which provide opportunity for cross-curricular study. The suggestions provided in this section and in the activity section which preceded this session, will allow you to cover the National Curriculum requirements of improvisation, exploration, refinement, developing mood and feeling, looking at contrasts, the organisation of dance into beginnings, middles and ends, and the use of cross-curricular themes. Traditional British Isles dances should also be included, as should dance from different times and places.

Each dance session should begin with a warm-up activity which should be, as far as possible, related to the dance topic. For example, if you are working on a fairground theme let the children warm-up by travelling around the room, rising and falling, stopping and starting, slowing down and changing direction.

• Playground – use various pieces of equipment found in a playground to suggest dance ideas. Musical stimuli could include: 'Theme from the

Filleted Place' by the Shadows and 'Háry János Suite' by Zoltán Kodály.

• Seashore – use as sources: waves, swirling water, shore life such as crabs and starfish to bring out ideas on paths and movement. Musical stimuli could include extracts from 'Fingals Cave' by Mendelssohn.

• Robots – this theme could be helpful in exploring tension and stuttering movement, perhaps leading to a total breakdown among the robots. Electronic movement could be used here. Musical stimuli could include 'Welcome to the Machine' from *Wish You Were Here* by Pink Floyd.

• The fairground – use the different rides found at the fair such as switchbacks, roller-coasters, dodgems, waltzers and helter-skelters to provide ideas. Fairground music could also be explored. Musical stimuli could include 'Monty Python's Flying Circus' from *BBC TV Themes*, 'Entry of the Gladiator' from *Great Marches of the World* (Decca) and 'Little Red Computer' from the BBC's *Let's Move* programme.

• Football – explore in dance the movements employed in a football match – such as tackling, running, falling,

heading, chesting, moving into position, passing and so on. Musical stimuli could include 'Match of the Day' from *BBC TV Themes*.

• Wild animals – let the children mime the movements of the different wild animals such as elephants, lions, tigers, snakes, giraffes, apes and others. Develop the mime into a dance; for example, the heavy plodding of an elephant might become a contrast to the light, sliding, slithering of a snake. Musical stimuli could include *Carnival of the Animals* by Saint-Saëns.

• The supermarket – go through the things that supermarket staff and shoppers do in a busy supermarket; for example, selecting and discarding goods, stacking shelves, lining up at the check-out and such like.

• The airport – explore what happens in a busy terminal; for example, buying tickets, getting on board the aircraft, reactions as the aeroplane takes off and so on.

• Fire! – pretend a fire engine arrives at the scene of a fire, fire fighters unroll hoses, reel up ladders, enter the blazing building....

• Dolls – imagine the dolls in a nursery come to life one night and move in their own particular ways. Musical stimuli may include *Coppélia* by Delibes, *Golliwog's*

Cakewalk by Debussy, 'Air' by Tomita from *Snowflakes are Dancing* (RCA).

• Fairy tales – use the plot from one of the well-known fairy tales such as 'Cinderella', 'Dick Whittington' and 'Jack and the Beanstalk' as the basis for a dance activity.

• The rush hour – use the theme of commuters going home at a busy street intersection, on foot and in cars.

• Traffic police – let the children pretend to direct traffic while others propel vehicles of different sorts – heavy transporters, milk floats, an old 'banger' breaking down and so on.

• Trial scenes – use trials from poems such as *Who killed Cock Robin?* or *Who stole the Tarts?* (see *Puffin Book of Nursery Rhymes*) as stimuli.

• A day by the sea – use this theme to explore all the different seaside themes such as sandcastles, vendors on the promenade, going into the sea, itinerant entertainers and such like.

• The marching band – each child can play different instruments and move in rhythm to what is being played.

• The circus – choose various circus performers such as clowns, ringmasters, acrobats, the human cannonball and so on. Musical stimuli could include 'Circus Band' by Merle Evans (Decca).

• Bird migration – explore the movement of an enormous flock of migrating birds –

flying, hovering, landing and making patterns in the sky.

• On parade! – the children can act like soldiers on parade – lining up, marching, drilling, fainting, charging and so on.

• The great machine – let the children pretend to be a component part of some vast machine, each child performing his own separate function, like a cog wheel, or gear.

• Hospital – explore busy hospital life with doctors, nurses, patients, visitors, ambulances, porters, and stretcher bearers.

• Board game – choose board games such as ludo, chess and snakes and ladders and let each child pretend to be a different part of the game.

• Free fall – explore the idea of jumping out of an aeroplane, falling quickly at first and then slowly as the parachute opens. The children can make patterns in the sky with other fallers.

• Earthquake – use the theme of being caught in an earthquake, running, hiding, dodging, falling, avoiding falling debris, picking the way around holes and so on.

• Accident – use the theme of a street accident with crowds gathering, ambulances

arriving, first aid being given, reactions of different members of the crowd and so forth.

• Spaceship lands – pretend a spaceship crashes to the earth. What sort of space people get out? How do they move around? How are they greeted by the local inhabitants?

• Police station – use a police station as a theme, with police officers, lost children, arrested criminals, people being put in the cells and so on.

• Street entertainers – use all the different types of street entertainers such as organ grinders, escapologists, musicians and so on.

• Power cut! – the lights go out, no one can see anything. The children can move carefully, finding ways of avoiding others.

• Building site – explore what building workers do, such as digging, excavating, building, knocking old buildings down, eating, resting, guiding vehicles and so on.

• Trapped! – what happens

when animals are caught in traps? The children can show fear, anguish, despair, attempts to escape and eventual release.

• Olympics! – go through all the events including the opening ceremony and medal presentations.

• Noah's ark – use the theme of Noah and his family rounding up the animals and then explore what happens when the animals enter the ark two by two to find homes on board.

• Skating – the children can move smoothly in different directions, skating well, performing intricate movements, skating badly and falling over.

• Assembly line – use the theme of working on an assembly line making a car. Each worker should have a different function, some are enthusiastic, some are bored. Musical stimuli could include *The Sorcerer's Apprentice* by Dukas, 'Mars' from *The Planets Suite* by Holst as well as music by Tangerine Dream and Jean Michel Jarre.

• Harvesting – explore what it is like going to work in the fields, gathering in the harvest, using different implements, carrying baskets, using machines and so on.

• The rodeo – explore all the aspects of a rodeo such as riding bucking horses, roping steers, performing tricks with lariats and the grand finale ride past.

• Shipwrecked! – use the theme of a storm at sea to explore such concepts as trying to maintain balance, being thrown overboard, struggling in water, clinging to wreckage and being washed ashore.

• Puppets – pretend to be marionettes dancing on the end of strings, getting caught in the strings and moving gracefully. What happens when the strings break?

• The orchestra – conduct different instruments at a concert. Show different moods, working up to a climax and finish by taking a bow.

• Camping – explore what happens when you go camping from arriving at the camp site, putting up tents and constructing a campfire, to gathering wood, cooking food, keeping tents down in storms and sleeping.

• Chickens in the farmyard – let the children run around like chickens – being fed, trying to get over and under a fence, fluttering when the dog barks and so on.

• Emotions – the children can work in groups. Each group can choose a different emotion as the basis for a dance, for example, happiness, fear, anger, depression and so on.

• Kitchen – use the theme of working in the kitchen of a large restaurant. Show cooks, waiters, washers-up, cleaners, the manager, triumphs and disasters.

• Babies – explore the theme of babies in a crèche. Show how they are unable to walk properly, crawling, tottering, falling over, getting up, trying to hurry, moving in an uncoordinated way and so on.

• Wasps! – move as if attacked by a swarm of wasps, running, diving, hiding, flicking and leaping.

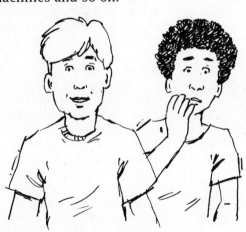

An indoor warm-up

Label the four walls of the hall
'north', 'south', 'east' and 'west'
respectively. Call out these
compass points and ask the
children to respond by
running to the relevant wall
and touching it. When they
have grasped the point of the
activity, start eliminating the
last two children to touch the
correct wall each time. These
children can then help you
spot the last two children in
subsequent rounds. Try to
make sure that no children are
left standing around and
getting cold for any length of
time.

An outdoor warm-up

Use any markings on the
playground or field for the
children to run round and
across. For example, on a
netball court get the children
to run along the lines of the
thirds markings and then
diagonally across the areas of
the thirds themselves (see
diagram). They could sprint
the diagonals.

Having done this initial
running, the children can form
pairs and run some

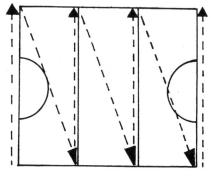

relay races. Depending on
their ages, the children could
run a third, a half, or even the
whole length of the pitch
before handing over to their
partners.

If the children will be using
a ball of a specific size in the
main part of the lesson, then
try to include work with the
ball in the warm-up. For
example, a suitable warm-up
might be to put the children
into groups of five or seven
and tell each group to stand in
a straight line, with about

1.5m between each child. Then
on the command 'go', the first
child in each group should
dribble or carry the ball in a
zigzag formation, slalom style,
between each of the other
children to the end of the line
and back again. When the child
reaches the front of the line
she should pass the ball to the
next child in the line. This
continues until all the children
in each team has had a go.

There are many other warm-
ups which incorporate skill
practices that can be used
before a games lesson. The
various associations and
governing bodies of different
sports often produce booklets
of such activities which can
easily be used or adapted.

Simple games skills

1. Throwing and catching

Age range
Four to five.

Group size
Individuals and pairs.

What you need
A large ball such as a football or netball.

What to do
If there are enough balls to go round, then the children should have one each.

However, this series of activities can easily be performed with the children working in groups of two or three. If they are sharing balls, the children should act as counters when they are not working.

Explain to the children the principle of bouncing a ball. They should push the ball to the ground with two hands, so that when it comes up again it bounces at about waist height. Go on to explain and demonstrate catching. The children must watch the ball at all times. They should grab at the ball and not expect it to bounce straight back into the hands. Tell them to spread their fingers and use their whole hand to catch the ball, not just their fingertips.

Once you have allowed the children some time to practise bouncing and catching a ball, ask them to do five bounces and catches in a row. Tell them that they will score one point for every completed catch, so that a final total of five is possible. Let them have the opportunity to improve on their final scores.

When most of the children seem to have grasped the idea of bouncing and catching tell them to form groups of two or three and introduce the concept of throwing and catching. (The children will use a bounce pass to maintain continuity with the previous work.) Demonstrate what is required. The ball should bounce about two thirds of the way between the children who stand about 3m apart so that the trajectory of the ball is upwards as the children receive and catch it. (This will provide the groundwork for later work on such games as netball.)

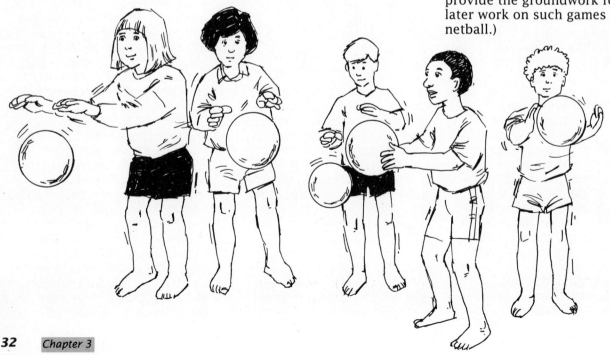

Ask the children to try and make consecutive passes and catches without dropping the ball. Remind them that the ball will not always come to them, and so sometimes they will have to move into position to receive the pass. When the children are able to make five consecutive passes they should try to do ten and so on.

2. Piggy-in-the-middle

Age range
Four to five.

Group size
Small groups of three or five.

What you need
A ball per group, preferably a size 5 football or netball.

What to do
The aim of this activity is to introduce the game 'piggy-in-the-middle'. However, you can set your own rules or maybe ask the children to help once they have had a go at the game. One rule that needs to be set from the outset is that players are not allowed to move when they are holding the ball.

If the children are working in groups of three adopt a two versus one situation, where one child stands between the other two players and tries to intercept the ball. Point out to the children that the child who is trying to intercept the ball should stand near to the player who is to receive the ball.

The children must use an overarm pass to throw the ball and it is a good idea for them to practise this before they start the game. The size of the children will indicate whether they will need to use one or two hands to throw the ball, although as the children grow older it will become a one handed throw. They need to hold the ball to one side of their heads, bend their knees and throw the ball upwards, at the same time straightening their knees.

If the children will be working in groups of five organise the groups so that there are two 'pigs' and three catchers. This version is slightly more complicated than when working in threes as it introduces the basic skills of marking and, to a lesser extent, dodging.

The only other rule to make, is that no child should touch any other player during the game.

3. Quoit relay

Age range
Four to five.

Group size
Small teams.

What you need
A variety of bats, balls, bean bags, quoits and hoops.

What to do
Ask the children to run 10m and use a large hoop at the end of the run to mark the distance. This way the children will know exactly where they have to run to.

Organise the children into teams and try to make sure that at least two of the teams are of the same number. Explain to the children that only one member from each team will be working at a time and that the others must wait their turn.

Give the first child in each team an object to hold such as a quoit. They must then run to the hoop, jump into it and run back to their teams, passing the quoits to the next child, and then sitting down. Each game finishes when all the children have had their turn and the whole team is sitting down.

Having explained what they have to do, don't be too dispirited if the children make an absolute mess of this the first few times they try it – they will eventually get the idea!

Once the children have mastered the idea of what they have to do, other actions can be introduced into the relay.
• The children can carry a ball to the hoop and bounce the ball in the hoop, catch it and then run back with it and pass it on to the next child in their team.
• The children can carry a bean bag on a bat to the hoop and then back again. If the bean bag is dropped the child must stop and put the bean bag back on to the bat before he can continue. The bat and bean bag are then passed to the next child in the team.
• A bean bag is put into the hoop for each member of the team. The first child then runs to pick up a bean bag and passes it to the next child in the team. The second child carries the bean bag to the hoop, picks up another one and carries the two bean bags back to the next child in the team. The game continues so that the last child to go from each team will carry three bean bags to the hoop, pick up the last bean bag and then run back to the team. The game finishes when all the bean bags

have been collected and the team is sitting down.

Many other types of games can be played using lots of different equipment. As the children get more proficient at the game more obstacles can be added; for example, skittles, which the children can weave in and out of, or new skills can be introduced such as dribbling a football.

4. Improving throwing and catching

Age range
Five to six.

Group size
Individuals, pairs and small groups.

What you need
A variety of balls, bean bags, quoits and hoops; chalk.

What to do
Set out some hoops so that each child in a pair stands either side of one hoop. Give each pair a ball and ask them to do a bounce pass to each other. As the children improve their throwing and catching, they should move further apart. The aim of the practice is for the children to complete ten consecutive catches. If the ball is dropped, they must start again.

Emphasise that the children should push the ball downwards as they bounce it, stepping as they do so. They should also spread their fingers and snatch the ball as they receive it.

Next, use chalk to draw some 1m diameter circles on a wall. In the middle of each circle draw and fill in a large bullseye. The children must then use a chest pass to throw a ball at the targets.

When doing a chest pass the children should spread their hands around the ball, which is held at chest height, and point their wrists at the target. They should step forward as they throw the ball.

Allow the children plenty of time to practise this technique. Once they have practised this throw, organise them into pairs and tell them that one of them will throw while the other will keep score. Tell the children that they must try to score as many points as possible in five throws. You can decide what the points will be; for example, five points for a bullseye and two if the ball hits inside the circle. There could also be a bonus point given if the ball is caught as it rebounds. The children should use a football when they first start the game, but use a smaller ball as they become more skilful. Make sure that all the children have a chance to throw the ball and keep score.

5. Small team games

Age range
Five to six.

Group size
Small teams (with an odd number of children in each team).

What you need
Footballs, a variety of bats, balls, bean bags, quoits, large hoops, marker disks or skittles.

What to do
Before you play the game it will be necessary to teach the children the basics of dribbling a football. To do this they must keep the ball near to their feet and move it by doing little pushes forward with the instep or outside of their feet. Make sure that the children use both feet.

Activity 1
Using the marker disks or skittles set out several 10m courses. Organise the children into teams and ask the first children in each team to dribble a ball in and out of the disks or skittles in both directions. (They must go in and out both there and back. This will stop the children pushing the football too far in front of them.) The game finishes when all the children have had a turn and the whole team is sitting down.

Activity 2
Use quoits for batons and organise a number of relay races in which the children must run, hop or skip. The races finish when all the children have had a turn and the whole team is sitting down.

Activity 3
Organise the children into teams of five or seven. One of the children in each team should hold a ball and stand facing the rest of the team. The other children should stand one behind the other about a metre away from the child with the ball. The child should then use either a chest, bounce or shoulder pass to pass the ball to the first child in her team who passes the ball back and runs to the back of the line.

This continues until the first child is at the front of the team again. The child with the ball must then put the ball on the ground and run to the back of the line. The first child then picks up the ball and repeats the game. The game finishes when all the children are back in their original starting positions.

This may seem a rather complicated game, but it is worth playing because it can be used over and over again throughout the children's schooling.

Activity 4
Organise the children into groups of five or seven and give each group a ball. Tell each group to stand in a circle with one child holding the ball in the middle. The idea of this game is that the children should develop speed and accuracy by chest passing the ball.

One of the children in the circle should stand outside the circle behind another child. He must then run round the outside of the circle while the ball is passed from the centre to each child who throws it back to the centre each time. The ball should be passed in the same direction as the child runs and the idea is that he must try and beat the ball. If the ball is dropped, the runner is the winner, and if the runner beats the ball back to the start position, then the runner also wins. The runner then becomes the thrower, and takes his position in the middle of the circle.

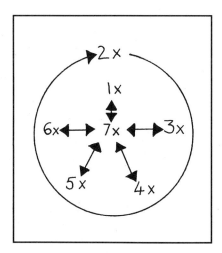

If the runner always beats the ball don't use a middle player, simply play the game by passing the ball round the circle.

This game can also be used with a variety of passes.

Short tennis

1. The grip

Age range
Six to seven.

Group size
Individuals, pairs and small teams.

What you need
Plastic rackets, bean bags, sponge balls.

What to do
Probably the simplest racket and ball game to introduce to the children is short tennis. This is simply a smaller version of tennis, but also involves other skills found in other games such as table tennis, badminton and squash.

To introduce the co-ordination which the children will need for the game and to give them an 'eye' for the ball the children will need to practise some simple racket and ball exercises. They will need to be taught the grip and the names of the racket parts.

Use plastic rackets as they will not be too heavy or unwieldy for young arms and hands. If the children do have problems with the weight of the racket they should hold the racket shaft nearer to the racket head, using the correct grip which is the 'shake hands' grip. This grip is common throughout racket sports so it is worth making sure that the children use it from the outset.

Tell the children to hold the racket shaft at the very top, near the head, using their non-playing hand. The actual face of the racket should be held sideways on to the child so that she cannot see the strings. The child then shakes hands with the racket handle using her playing hand. She should find that she makes a

'V' shape with her thumb and index finger, which is in line with the head of the racket (see diagram). The non-playing hand should remain at the neck of the racket, loosely holding it.

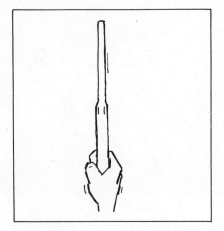

To practise this grip the children can use a bean bag and play a team game. This will get the children used to holding their rackets without putting them under any pressure to control a ball. Sort out teams of even numbers and split them so that half the players stand at one end of the course and the rest at the other end. The course should be about 10m in length.

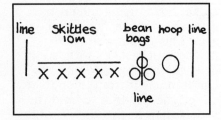

Give one child in each team a bean bag. This child must then run across to his team-mates while carrying the bean bag on his racket. If he drops the bean bag he must pick it up and put it back on to his racket before he can continue.

When he reaches the other side he should pass the bean bag to another child who should run back with it on her racket until all the children have had a go. Make sure the children only use one hand to hold the racket (they can put their 'spare' hand behind their backs). They should use the correct grip, but with the back of the hand facing downwards so that the racket looks somewhat like a frying pan (see diagram.)

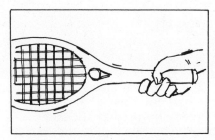

At the end of the lesson let the children cool-down by playing some small team-games. Set out a row of five skittles or markers, so that they stretch for about 10m. At the end of the markers place three bean bags on a chalked line and place a large hoop about 3m away. Draw a chalk line at the end of the hoop. Obviously the number of skittles and the distance between the various obstacles will depend on the size of the area.

The team sizes can vary, but teams of four or five will probably work best. This course is fairly simple in that the first child in each team should dribble the football in and out of the skittles, stop the ball on the line where the bean bags are, throw the bean bags into the hoop, run to the line at the end, touch it and run back to the start. On the way back the children must replace the bean bags and pick

up the ball which they should then pass to the next child in their teams. All three bean bags must be in the hoop before the child can go on. The team which has all its members back at the start line, with the bean bags replaced and the football in the hands of one of the team, is the winner.

2. The forehand

Age range
Six to seven.

Group size
Individuals, pairs and small groups.

What you need
Short-tennis rackets, sponge tennis-sized balls, various equipment for team games.

What to do
As this session may tend to be fairly static it is best carried out indoors or, if played outdoors, done during the summer.

Ideally, each child should be given a racket and ball. Where this is not possible the children can work with partners, but anything above this number will become tedious for the children.

Start the session by reminding the children of the correct racket grip, then check each child's grip. Next, teach the children the 'ready' position. Tell them to pretend to face an imaginary net, bend their knees and hold their rackets at waist height, with their non-playing hands at the throat of the racket gently supporting it. The reason for doing this is that in a game they will not know on which side the ball is going to

approach them and so they must be ready to hit the ball on either side.

Once they are standing in the ready position and holding the racket with the correct grip, they can be taught the swing action needed for a forehand stroke. (For simplicity, the following explanation is given for a right-handed player. However, left-handed actions are simply the reverse of the right-handed ones.)

From the ready position the child should turn to the right, stepping across to the right with his left leg sideways on to the net. At the same time he should take his racket back so that the head (top) of the racket is level with his right shoulder. He should then swing through so that the head of the racket is level with his waist and then 'follow through' until he ends up with the racket level with his left shoulder. This 'follow-through' has a bearing on the path the ball will take, so it is a very important feature to stress. The children should then

return to the ready position. The ball will be struck as the racket swings through level with the waist (see diagram).

Go through this action several times with the children until the vast majority of them have got the idea. You can then get out the sponge balls and let the children have a go. If they are working on their own, they will need to hold the ball in their non-playing hand.

On reaching the part in the stroke where they have stepped across to the right and have their rackets up at shoulder height (see diagram), they should hold the ball out at arms length and then bounce it level with their front foot. The ball should bounce back up at about waist height and level with the front foot, about a racket length away from the children.

ask the children to count the number of strokes in each rally and see which pair completes the most. If the ball bounces twice or the rally is interrupted in any way the counting must start again.

3. The backhand

Age range
Six to seven.

Group size
Individuals and pairs.

What you need
Short-tennis rackets, sponge balls.

What to do
Teach the children how to do a backhand shot. Basically, all the teaching points are the same as for the forehand except when it comes to the positioning of the body. The child should step across with her right foot so that her right shoulder is facing towards an imaginary net (see diagram).

When practising backhand shots with balls the children will have to work in pairs as it is very difficult to feed the ball to oneself.

At the same time as they drop the balls, the children should start to swing their rackets, keeping their eyes on the ball rather than the rackets. Remind them that they must follow through with their racket at the end of the swing so that the ball goes straight ahead.

If they find that the ball keeps going to the side, this may mean that they are not following through correctly. If they keep missing the ball this could mean that they are not watching the ball properly. Another reason why they may miss the ball is that the ball may not be at the right height. If this is the case they may find it easier to have a partner drop the ball for them.

If the children are working in pairs then one child should stand to the racket side (in case of a right-handed hitter the 'feeder' stands to the right of the hitter). The feeder then holds the ball out at arms length, but ready to step back once the ball has been dropped. Ideally, it should land level with the hitter's front foot and bounce at waist height, about a racket length away from the hitter. (The teaching points for the hitter are the same as above in the individual practice.)

Whichever method of feeding the ball is used, it is important to impress on the children the need to use a smooth hitting action rather than 'thrashing' at the ball.

Further activity
Once the children have grasped the basic idea of how to hit a forehand, and it may take some time and patience, you can introduce the idea that the children must follow through with their shots or they will be forever picking up the ball from the ground. Tell the children to work in pairs to produce a rally. They should start the rally in the same way as before, but hit the ball towards a partner. It should be stressed that there is no need for them to hit the ball hard and that, at the beginning, they should aim to hit the ball slightly upwards.

If you want to make this practice a little competitive

One important teaching point, particularly applicable to the backhand, is that the children should stand away from the ball so that they can have a nice easy swing. If they are too close to the ball they will find it difficult to swing at all. Remind them of the importance of the follow-through.

Having been given plenty of time to practise this stroke the children can attempt to have a rally using both forward and backhand drives.

4. The volley, overhead and smash

Age range
Six to seven.

Group size
Individuals and pairs.

What you need
Short-tennis rackets, sponge balls.

What to do
Once the children are quite proficient at hitting the ball when it has bounced, you can begin to teach them the forehand and backhand volley, where the ball is not allowed to bounce. The volley action is one of 'punching' the ball and involves little follow through with the racket.

Finally, the overhead shot and the smash need to be taught. For the overhead shot the ball must be, as the name suggests, high and overhead. The child should take the racket back above his head, keeping his elbows bent so that the racket is tipped backwards. As the child makes contact with the ball the elbow is straightened – there is no follow-through.

For the smash the ball again needs to be high, but in front of the body so that the child can step into the action, just as with the forehand ground stroke. After the ball has been hit, the follow-through leaves the racket head near the left knee on the forehand smash, and near the right knee on a backhand one. As the name suggests, the smash involves some aggression, whereas the overhead shot is really more of a defensive stroke.

Allow the children plenty of time to practise these shots. They can work in pairs with one child feeding the ball to the other child using an underarm throw and throwing the ball high.

5. Scoring

Age range
Six to seven.

Group size
Pairs.

What you need
Short-tennis rackets, sponge balls.

What to do
The children now need to be taught how the scoring for short tennis works. The

scoring system is the same as in table-tennis in that each player has five serves at a time. However, both the server and receiver can score. The scores are always announced so that the server's score is said first. Set your own winning score, but whatever you decide on, you must allow each server to have the same number of serves. For example, you might decide that the first child to reach 11 or above is the winner. This would mean that each child would have 10 serves with the final scores something like 20-0, 11-9, 4-16 or 15-5.

As primary schools are generally limited in the amount of space they have available, you might decide to organise a session so that for each pair playing another does the scoring.

Once the children have grasped the rudiments of scoring in singles, doubles may be introduced. Here the play is basically the same as in singles except that children play side by side with a partner. You may decide to impose the rule that the children play their side of the court to stop one child 'hogging' the ball, but you should point out that the children must 'call' if the ball is in between them so that there are no clashes of rackets.

When playing doubles, the order of scoring goes so that the first child to serve is followed by the first child on the other team, who is followed by the second child in the first team to serve, followed by the last child. The very first serve is always done by the player on the right of the court. It doesn't matter which pair has the first set of five serves; if there is any dispute they should toss a coin to decide. (Make sure the children swap sides of the court so that each child has the opportunity to receive serve.)

If there is room, the proper game of short tennis is played on a badminton court with a net set at 83cm at each end and 78cm in the middle. The whole court is used.

Rounders

In this section the children will be taught the basics of throwing, catching, bowling and batting to enable them to play a small game of indoor rounders.

1. Playing indoors

Age range
Seven to eight.

Group size
Individuals, pairs and small teams.

What you need
Rounders bats, sponge or plastic balls, mats, posts, markers.

What to do
Divide the class in half and tell the children which half will be batting and which will be fielding. They will now need to practise catching the ball, which in this case is a sponge ball. Ask the children from each side to get into pairs and give each pair a ball. Ask them to stand about a metre away from their partners and throw the balls underarm to each other. The thrower's arm

should follow through the throwing action so that it ends up pointing at the child to whom she is throwing the ball. (This action will be used in bowling both indoors and out.)

The child who receives the ball must stretch out her hand towards it and make sure that her body is behind the ball. This is important because she is less likely to drop the ball if she does this. She must also watch the ball at all times. As it gets within reach she must snatch the ball out of the air, and not wait for it to come to her.

Once the children are quite good at catching from this distance (for example, when they catch ten consecutive throws) they can move so that they stand 3m apart.

Move on to look at batting. If the children are working indoors there will be a limit on the space available, so you will only be able to show the children how to do the action, and they will have to practise it during the game. Tell them that, as in throwing, they must watch the ball right from when it leaves the thrower's hands. They should stand sideways on to the ball so that the bat is back near to their shoulder (see diagram).

As the ball gets nearer to them they should then start to swing the bat. It is difficult to say exactly when that will be, because it varies from person to person and is largely a matter of practice.

Set out a pitch which resembles the one shown below. Obviously the size of the pitch will vary, but you need to allow space for the runners to run around the outside of the mats.

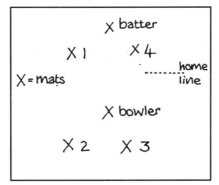

The batters must stand on their mat and they have three attempts in which to hit the ball. If they hit the ball they must run. They have to run round the outside of each marker until they cross the home line. If the batter is made 'out' then she must run with the next batter until this batter is out. This means that if all bar one batter are out then the whole team will be running with that one child. If more than one child is running, it is the last child to cross over the home line who determines whether or not the batter is in or out. Each time the batter crosses the line a rounder is scored so, for example, if the batter has two runners with him and they all get home, only one rounder is scored.

In the fielding team there should be one back stop, one

bowler (you might want to bowl when the children first start playing the game), four fielders (one on each mat), and the rest spread out around the room – making sure that they do not get in the way of the batters when they are running. The batter can be made out by being caught, or if the fielding team manage to pass the ball from the first mat to the fourth mat before the batter has crossed the home line. In this case, the ball is fielded and thrown to the first mat and then thrown round the mats in order. If the ball is dropped *en route* then it must go back to the first mat and start again.

If the children are only just starting to play you may have to say that the children are allowed to drop the ball once before it has to go back to the first mat, or the mats could be moved closer together, while leaving the home line where it is.

This game can be very noisy so give a bonus rounder to the quietest team at the end of the game.

2. Playing outdoors: throwing overarm

Age range
Seven to eight.

Group size
Pairs and two teams.

What you need
Rounders balls, bats, posts.

What to do
Before starting to play rounders the children must be taught how to catch and throw overarm. Organise them into

pairs and give each pair a rounders ball. Tell them to stand about a metre apart and use an underarm throw to throw and catch the ball. It should be stressed that when throwing a ball underarm the children should follow through the movement, once the ball has left their hand, so that the hand is pointing where they want the ball to go. (This will be the way they will bowl the ball in the game.)

The catcher must snatch the ball out of the air. He should move so that his body is behind the ball so that if he misses the ball it will hit him and so he will stand a chance of fumbling a catch at least! The catcher must catch the ball 'into' his body. This will serve two purposes – it takes the sting out of the ball and it will make the catch more secure.

As the children get better at catching and throwing they should move further apart, up to say 3m, before they stop. Ask the children to complete ten consecutive passes at a metre before they move to the 3m distance.

Once the the children have practised throwing underarm, they will be able to move on to throwing overarm. Before they start, however, you need to make them aware of the following two rules:
• No one may throw a ball until they are told to;
• No one should fetch a ball until they are told to.

Impress on the children that these rules are not to be broken; they are set for their own safety. This will be good practice for the future when they will begin to use such things as javelins!

Organise the children into pairs and provide each pair with a ball, then line them up so that the ones without balls stand well behind the line of throwers. Show the children how to throw the ball. Tell them to hold the ball in their

hands so that their palms are facing upwards. The balls should be near their ears on their throwing sides, and their weight taken further back. They should then whizz their arms through in a bent position and throw the ball upwards as, at the same time, their weight moves forwards. Their arms then follow through so that they end up near their left knees (if they are right-handed).

Once the first group of children have all thrown their balls they must go and collect them and let the other children have a throw. Move the children so that each child is standing about 5m away from her partner. The two lines should face each other, but be spaced well apart. If space is short put the pairs into groups and have only one group working at a time.

Afterwards, the children can practise the overarm throw, throwing a ball at their partners who must try to catch it. Stress that they will most likely have to move in order to catch the ball correctly. As they get better at making two-handed catches you might want to add the constraint that they are only allowed to catch with one hand.

3. Playing outdoors: batting and bowling

Age range
Seven to eight.

Group size
Pairs and two teams.

What you need
Rounders balls, bats, posts (two per team).

What to do
Let the children revise the underarm throw used in the previous activity's catching and throwing practice. To do this they will need to work in pairs, with a bat and ball between them. One child in each pair must be the bowler and use the underarm throw, while the other one stands with the bat, sideways on to the bowler and about 5m away. The batter needs to hold the bat ready (so that it is back and up level with her shoulder).

She must watch the ball as it leaves the bowler's hand and, as it gets near, swing the bat and hit it. The batter must follow through this hitting action so that the bat ends up over her left shoulder (if she is right-handed). The batters and bowlers should swap places so that they each have a go at being batter and bowler. (**NB:** Make sure that the pairs are not too close together.)

Once the children have been allowed some time to practise batting and bowling they can start to play a game. Begin with two teams of four. One team should be the batting side while the other consists of a bowler, a post fielder and two out fielders.

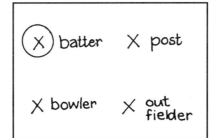

The batter must run around the post to score a rounder, although she is allowed to stop at the post if there is another batter. The fielding team can get the batters out by catching the hit or by touching the post with the ball before the batter reaches it. The batter is allowed two misses when she is batting. If she misses the third she is out. Once a batter is out she should continue running with other batters as described in the indoor version (see page 43). When the children get better at hitting, throwing and catching, the numbers of children on each team can be gradually increased to include a back stop until there is a full team of nine.

Further activity
Once you are satisfied that the children have enough skill, which may not be during this year, they could start playing other classes or local schools in matches.

NB: The rules for rounders are listed in the official rule book. They have not been listed here as they are occasionally changed.

Football

When all the children are fairly competent at using all the football skills and techniques, they can begin to play simplified games of six-a-side football under supervision.

1. Ball control

Age range
Eight to nine.

Group size
Individuals and pairs.

What you need
6m × 6m mats, footballs.

What to do
Ask the children to stand on a mat and throw a ball into the air. They should use any parts of their bodies to keep the ball in the air. How many times can they bounce the ball like this?

Let the children repeat this exercise but this time they can use any parts of their bodies, except their hands or arms.

Having let the children practise this by themselves, ask them to work in pairs in marked squares of about 10m. How long can both children keep the ball in the air between them, using any parts of their bodies except their hands or arms?

2. Dribbling a football

Age range
Eight to nine.

Group size
Individuals.

What you need
Balls of varying sizes, obstacles such as bean bags, cones and so on.

What to do
Teach and demonstrate the skill of running with a football while keeping it under control. As you run the ball should be

tapped from the inside of one foot to the inside of the other foot. At first the children should do this slowly, but gradually they can do it with increasing speed. Let the children practise this with a variety of different shaped balls. Make sure that they do not kick the ball too far ahead. Those children who find mastering this skill difficult should be allowed to walk with the ball at their feet.

As the children gain in confidence allow them to dribble the ball in and out of a number of stationary objects such as bean bags, skittles, hoops and so on.

Repeat this exercise but ask the children to change speed as you shout various commands such as 'walk', 'run slowly' and 'run quickly'.

Ask the children to dribble the ball while they run slowly, but changing direction at the commands 'left', 'right' and so on. Repeat this exercise at ever-increasing speeds.

At the command 'go' ask the children to kick the ball ahead of themselves, run after it, get it under control and start dribbling it.

End the lesson with a number of games based on the skills being practised. Put the children in teams and organise relay races, with one child in each team at a time dribbling the ball through obstacles and returning the ball to the next child and so on.

When the children reach a sufficient standard they could be asked to turn occasionally and run backwards while still controlling the ball.

Put the children in pairs in marked squares, about 10m × 10m. How long can one child dribble the ball within the square before she is dispossessed by her partner?

3. Acceleration and deceleration

Age range
Eight to nine.

Group size
Individuals.

What you need
Footballs or balls of football size.

What to do
Ask the children to run slowly until they hear the command 'change!' On this they must accelerate and run as fast as they can, making sure that they do not bump into anyone else. On hearing the command 'change' the children should decelerate and run slowly, until you tell them to stop. Ask the children to run again, shout out various shapes such as 'squares', 'circles' and so on, and let the children make these shapes on the ground.

Ask the children to stand in a group. At the command of 'spaces' each child must run into a space and stand still.

Ask the children to run in straight lines, changing direction at the command of 'left', 'right', 'forward' and 'backwards'.

At the command 'move!' the children should run and jump, changing direction by 180°. They should run into a space and jump as high into the air as they can, landing with bent knees.

As the children become more confident, repeat most of these exercises, allowing the children to use balls, dribbling them at their feet.

4. Shooting

Age range
Eight to nine.

Group size
Individuals and pairs.

What you need
Footballs or balls of a similar size, a goal or a goal marked on a wall.

What to do
Teach and demonstrate the technique of shooting with the ball. The shooter should place her non-kicking foot alongside the ball. She should draw back her shooting foot and kick 'through' the ball, following through the movement in the direction the ball is intended to go. If the ball is struck in the middle the effect should be to keep the ball down.

Allow the children to have plenty of practice at shooting at goal or against a goal marked out on a wall. Roll a ball to each child, calling out his name, and ask the child to kick the ball straight off, with no controlling movement. Then put the children into pairs, and ask one child in each pair to roll the ball along the ground so that the other child can shoot at a target. Make sure that all the children have the opportunity to roll the ball and shoot at goal.

5. Heading the ball

Age range
Eight to nine.

Group size
Individuals and pairs.

What you need
Balloons or large soft balls such as footballs or balls of similar size.

What to do
Warm-up by playing a game of 'heading'. Suspend balloons or large soft balls from a line just over the children's heads. Allow them to run freely and then on your command 'head' they must leap and head a balloon.

Teach and demonstrate the technique of heading a ball downwards. As the ball comes through the air the header should run forward to meet it. He should try to make contact just above the middle of the ball, reaching the ball at the highest part of the jump. He should combine the force of his head, neck and body down on to the top half of the ball.

Having demonstrated the technique, arrange the children in a circle around you. Call out each child by name and throw a ball into the air. The child should run forward and head the ball back into your hands.

Organise the children into pairs and ask one child in each pair to throw the ball into the air while the other heads it down back towards the thrower. Make sure that all the children practise throwing and heading the ball.

6. Tackling

Age range
Eight to nine.

Group size
Pairs.

What you need
Footballs or balls of a similar size.

What to do
You will need to choose one of the children or another adult to help you demonstrate the technique of tackling a player and winning possession of the ball. The player with the ball should dribble it at a controlled speed. The tackling player should approach her opponent from the side, forcing him away. She should then attempt to place her foot under the ball when her opponent has the least amount of control over it, and attempt to lift it over her opponent's foot, thus dispossessing him.

This is a difficult manoeuvre, but an essential part of any player's armoury. Divide the children into pairs and allow them to spend most of this session attempting to make tackles, while you supervise them.

7. Chipping

Age range
Eight to nine.

Group size
Individuals, pairs and small groups of three.

What you need
Footballs or balls of a similar size.

What to do
Warm-up by asking the children to run in groups of three, passing a football from one child to another.

Teach and demonstrate the action of 'chipping' a ball, or making it rise in the air in a controlled fashion. The player should place his non-kicking foot at the side of the ball and bring his kicking foot down sharply on to the ball, producing a 'backspin' effect.

As the ball rises, he should withdraw his foot and then meet the ball again underneath it, thus chipping it into the air.

This technique will take quite a bit of individual practice, but when the children have gained sufficient confidence they should be allowed to practise chipping the ball over a raised object. If the session is taking place outside you could use the crossbar of a goal, or if indoors you could use a raised bar. Ask the children to stand about 4m away from the goal or bar at first; as they gain in skill they can move closer and closer, using an increasing amount of backspin to get the over the bar.

Organise the children into pairs. One child in each pair should try to chip the ball over the head of his partner when standing at varying distances from him.

Finally, the children can be placed in threes with one child standing between the other two. The two on either side can then try to chip the ball to one another, passing it over the child in the middle.

8. Throwing

Age range
Eight to nine.

Group size
Pairs and small teams.

What you need
Footballs or balls of a similar size.

What to do
Let the children warm-up by playing a game of 'follow-my-thumb'. Tell them to run around the area, but warn them to keep one eye on you. You should then indicate the direction in which the children must run with your thumb.

Demonstrate the throw-in technique. The thrower should spread her hands so that they are behind the ball and hold it behind her head. She should place her feet on an imaginary line. The aim of the throw-in is to throw the ball in a controlled manner as far as possible, while observing the laws of the game. She should swing her back and legs backwards in order to enable her to 'whip' forward with enough impetus to propel the ball a good distance. She must *not* move her feet as the ball leaves her hand.

Place the children in pairs and let them practise throwing the ball correctly to one another. As they gain confidence and skill, allow them to move farther and farther apart. However, do not let them strain too much in an attempt to gain distance. Good style and confidence are the objectives to be sought.

When the children have had ample opportunity to practise this technique, organise them into teams of about six. Each team should form a circle and one child should stand in the middle of each. The children on the edge of the circle must try to throw the ball to one another in the approved manner, without moving their

feet. Meanwhile, the child in the centre must try to intercept the ball as it is thrown across the circle. If she is successful then she rejoins the circle while the child who threw the ball replaces her in the centre of the circle and the game resumes.

9. Passing a football with the inside of the foot

Age range
Eight to nine.

Group size
Individuals and pairs.

What you need
Footballs or balls of a similar size; chalk.

What to do
Let the children warm-up by playing a game of 'bean bags'. Ask the children to run in pairs, each pair passing a bean bag from one to the other. If the bean bag is dropped both children are out.

Teach and demonstrate the technique of passing a ball using the inside of the foot. The non-kicking foot should be kept level with the ball at the moment of contact and it should be turned at the moment of impact to bring the inside of the foot against the middle of the ball firmly. Mark a 2m-wide area on a wall. The children can then practise passing the ball so that it strikes the wall within this space.

Tell the children to start with a stationary ball placed several metres from the wall. Each child in turn should run and make the pass without stopping. When most children can accomplish this with ease, place a ball 4m from the wall, then 6m and finally 10m.

Repeat this exercise, but this time you should roll the ball to the child as he starts to run. Allow the child to touch the ball once to control it and then make the pass with the second touch. As the children become more proficient, extend the distance to 1m, 6m and then 10m from the wall.

Finally, organise the children into pairs. One child in each pair should roll the ball to their partners. The second child should control the ball with one movement and pass it at the wall with the second. Make sure that the children regularly change roles.

10. Passing a football with the outside of the foot

Age range
Eight to nine.

Group size
Individuals and pairs.

What you need
Footballs or balls of a similar size, a hoop, chalk.

What to do
Teach and demonstrate the technique of passing a ball using the outside of the foot in an area marked out as for the previous activity. The child passing the ball should place her non-kicking foot so that it is slightly behind the ball at the moment of impact. She should turn her kicking foot slightly inwards to bring it into contact with the middle of the ball.

Having demonstrated the technique you can let the children repeat the exercises they carried out in the previous activity.

11. The long, high pass

Age range
Eight to nine.

Group size
Individuals, pairs and small teams.

What you need
Footballs or balls of a similar size, skittles.

What to do
Demonstrate and teach the techniques of the long, high pass. The kicker should run up to the ball, placing his non-kicking foot to the side of the ball and a little behind it. To make sure that the ball rises, he should strike the bottom of the ball with his kicking foot. The kicking foot should carry all the way through the movement to ensure direction and length, ending up in the direction that the ball is meant to go.

Let the children practise kicking the ball, in this fashion, towards a line marked with skittles about 10m away.

When the children can reach the line three out of five times, increase the distance to 15m, then 20m and finally 25m.

Repeat this exercise, but this time the children can work in pairs, making long, high passes to one another.

Finally, organise the class into teams. Each child in a team is allowed three passes to reach a line 25m away. For every ball that comes down within a metre of the line, the child gets one point. The team with the most number of points wins the game.

12. Trapping the ball with the sole of the foot

Age range
Eight to nine.

Group size
Individuals and pairs.

What you need
Footballs or balls of a similar size.

What to do
Teach and demonstrate the skill of trapping the ball with the sole of the foot. The person trapping the ball should respond to a lob by getting behind the ball's flight and moving smoothly towards the area of the ground where it should land. She should extend the sole of one foot towards the approaching ball and trap it with the sole, making a wedge between the boot and the ground, in a triangular shape.

Lob a ball to each child three or four times to let the class practise this movement. Then divide the children into pairs and place them so that they stand about 6m away from their partners. One child should lob a ball while the other tries to trap it. As the children become more accomplished, increase the distance between them.

13. The goalkeeper's dive

Age range
Eight to nine.

Group size
Individuals and pairs.

What you need
Footballs or balls of football size, mats.

What to do
Let the children warm-up by playing 'Goalkeeper'. Tell them to run freely, but to imagine that they are goalkeepers making a save, high and to one side, leaping in that direction.

Teach and demonstrate the goalkeeper's dive, using thick mats if the lesson takes place indoors. The move starts with a controlled spring to the side, *not* a flop on to the ball. It is essential that the children protect themselves from the ball by using their hands and body. As soon as their hands touch the ball they should bring it in to their bodies for extra protection. If the ball is too far away, an attempt should be made to deflect it by stretching out their arms.

Place the children in pairs and ask one child in each pair to throw the ball towards her partner. This child should make a goalkeeper's leap and try to stop the ball.

As the children grow more proficient the feeder child can kick the ball instead of throwing it. However, ensure that these kicks are not too powerful.

14. Crab football

Age range
Eight to nine.

Group size
Small groups of five.

What you need
Large soft balls (about the same size as a football), skittles.

What to do
Crab football is usually played indoors, although it can be played on a field. The game is played with teams of five children, although any number from three up to ten is possible if there is sufficient space.

Set out pairs of skittles for goals. The children can then play the game by sitting on their bottoms, with their hands, palms downwards, at their sides. They can only move on their bottoms, balanced by their hands.

To start the game throw the ball into the middle of the pitch. The children should then scuttle towards it. They are only allowed to touch the ball with their feet and the object of the game is to score a goal by kicking the ball between the skittles.

Netball

Netball can be taught to both sexes and there are similarities between netball and basketball.

The following are a number of warm-ups for netball which can be used for all the activities in this section.

• Ask the children to line up along the goal-line. They should run and touch the first line of the court, and run back to the goal-line, then run to the second line and back to the goal-line.

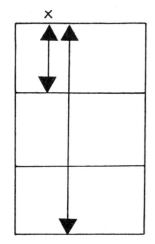

• Ask the children to jog and sprint in a zigzag pathway across the court. They should jog the straights and sprint the diagonals.

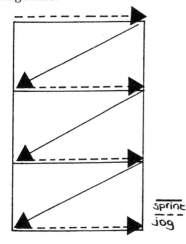

• Ask the children to sprint the length of the court and then walk back. They should repeat this three times. They might also like to race a partner.

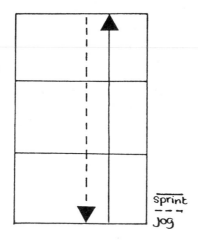

• Ask the children to run around the court. They should jog the short lines and sprint the long lines.

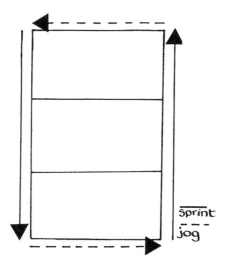

• Ask the children to jog sideways, backwards and forwards. Shout out the different directions and also signal them with your arms.
• Ask the children to run as a class. It is best if you lead the children and, if you do, tell the children that no one is allowed to overtake you. (If you do not want to run then stand in the centre circle of the court and let the children run round the outside of the court.)

Before they start to run the children should be told that if you shout 'one', then they must touch the ground to their right. If you shout 'two', then they must touch the ground to their left. If you shout 'three', then they must jump and land on one foot and then use the other foot to help them pivot round. If you shout 'four' then the children must shout back 'can we do a press up please?' You can either respond by saying 'yes' or 'no'. When they all moan, as they surely will, when you tell them that they *can* do a press up, you can respond by saying that they asked to do one! The children usually enjoy this last exercise.

1. Throwing and catching

Age range
Eight to nine.

Group size
Individuals, pairs and groups of three.

What you need
Netball courts, post, netballs.

What to do
The children will need to revise the throwing and catching skills they worked on in previous years. By now, hopefully, they should have a fair degree of skill, however, it is important to continue with skill practice. Keep to some of the familiar practices so that the children feel they are succeeding, but also introduce some new ones.

Teach children how to do a shoulder pass. To do this correctly the child should stand with his feet apart, with his left foot slightly in front of his right (for a right-handed player). He should hold the ball on his palm and help to balance it with his left hand. The ball should be in line with his right ear at shoulder level and his knees should be slightly bent. The aim is to push the ball up and forwards so that it goes in a loop. This pass will be used in the game to get the ball over a group of players or for shooting.

Let the children practise this particular throw by playing 'piggy-in-the-middle'. The 'pig' should stand with her arms stretched up above her head and the thrower must try to get the ball over her to his team-mate.

After the children have played this for a while, point out that to intercept the ball the 'pig' needs to be nearer to the receiver than the thrower,

so that they intercept the ball when it is coming down, rather than at its peak.

The children can also use this throw in a shooting practice. Organise the children into pairs. Each child can take five shots at goal, scoring one point every time they are successful. Can they get more points than their partner?

2. Marking

Age range
Eight to nine.

Group size
Individuals, pairs and groups of three.

What you need
Netball courts, posts, netballs.

What to do
There are two ways of marking an opponent who does not have the ball – face to face and side marking.

Start off by explaining the technique of side marking to

the children. Ask the children to choose partners and stand one in front of the other, both facing the same way. To begin with, the child standing behind should just act as a 'body', but once the children have been taught to dodge they can bring this technique into practice.

The marker is the child who is in front of her opponent. She should stand close to her opponent but must not touch him. By standing close together the marker will be able to sense what her opponent is doing. She should stand with her arms out to her side so making a bigger obstacle for her opponent to get round. (Remind the children that netball is a non-contact game.) Her knees should be slightly bent and she should stand on the balls of her feet rather than flat footed; ready to move in any direction. The marker needs to see her opponent, so she must look over one shoulder. Having established this position, the child who is standing behind (the opponent) should begin to move around the playing area while the marker must try to stay with him.

Next, demonstrate the technique of face to face marking. This time, as the name suggests, the children should face each other. The marker's position is exactly the same as in side marking, except that she need not look over her shoulder!

This type of marking has its limitations in that it is great for stopping the opponent getting the ball, but it does mean that the marker has no idea what is happening behind her; her team may be scoring a goal for all she knows! However, it is especially effective when used in the circle and at the centre pass.

When marking a player who has the ball you will need to introduce the 1m (3ft) rule. This states that if the opponent has the ball the marker must be at least 1m away from his landing foot. (As landing has not yet been covered, you should tell the children that they must be at least 1m from the front foot.) Show the children exactly how far 1m is, so that they have a clearer idea of the distance.

When teaching this technique to begin with, ask the opponent to stand behind a line as he would in a throw-in. The marker needs to be 1m away with her knees slightly bent and her arms outstretched towards the ball. She must shadow the ball, but make no contact with it or with her opponent as he moves it around.

Introduce the idea of leaning forwards towards the ball. To do this the marker needs to stand on one leg – still 1m away – and lean towards her opponent, stretching out one arm. This will help the marker to get nearer to the ball while still standing the correct distance

away. If she overbalances and moves nearer to her opponent than the permitted 1m she must move back quickly. This leaning type of marking is used most often in the circle for marking the shooters.

Let the children practise this form of marking in threes, so that one child is against the other two who have possession of the ball.

3. Dodging

Age range
Eight to nine.

Group size
Pairs and small groups.

What you need
Netball court, posts, netballs.

What to do
Once the children understand the concept of marking you can introduce the skill of dodging so that they can deal with being marked. The idea of dodging is to trick your marker. As with marking, the dodger should keep on the balls of his feet with his knees

slightly bent. The movement, or feinting, involves the upper part of the body. The dodger should start to go one way, using his upper body alone, and then run off in the opposite direction. As he runs, the child points in the direction he is going so that his team-mate with the ball knows where to send it. (It is important that this gesture is only seen by his team-mate, and not the opponent. Therefore, it should be kept at waist level and involve the lower arm only.)

The dodging itself must be quick and decisive, as the team-mate who has the ball only has three seconds in which to throw it once she has caught the ball. The children will probably dance around to start with and so it will be necessary for you to remind them exactly what they are supposed to be doing.

It is also possible to do a double feint, in other words to feint one way, then the other and finally run off in the direction originally feinted.

A dodger need not only go sideways, he can also move backwards away from the marker. He can use a feint as well, if he wants to, but it is not always necessary. To signal to his team-mate that he is going backwards he should point over his shoulder or head.

If dodgers are to be successful in outwitting their markers they must use the different feints and dodges with variety.

If the opponent is using face-to-face marking the dodger will have more trouble dodging his marker. He can try feinting in order to wrong foot his opponent and he can also try standing still and then making a sudden break – running sideways and then forwards, taking care not to make contact with his marker. Hopefully, this manoeuvre will take his opponent by surprise and mean that she is no longer facing the dodger. The dodger's team-mate should then throw the ball to the non-marked side of the dodger.

The children can work on practising dodging and marking in pairs without a ball initially. Then they can get into threes so that the marker can mark the player who does not have the ball. Finally, they can work in fours, two children versus two children, using a third of the court and chalk circles on the sidelines as goals. A bounce in the circle will count as a goal. As only 12 children can work on one court, the other children can work in pairs and threes and practise at the side of the court.

4. Situation marking and dodging

Age range
Eight to nine.

Group size
Individuals and small groups.

What you need
Netball court, netballs.

What to do
In this activity the children will practise face-to-face marking and dodging in a set situation taken from a game scenario. The scenario used is a centre pass which is set up so that the players in the team who have possession of the ball must get into the centre third of the court and receive the ball. The other team must try to stop them getting into this space by face-to-face marking.

If their opponents do manage to get into the third they must try to stop them receiving the pass.

The ball starts off with the centre who only has three seconds to make the pass from when the whistle is blown.

If the children are going to practise this on their own, the centre from the team who do not have the ball, should start the game by saying 'Play'. Once one team has had a go with the ball, the other team should have a go.

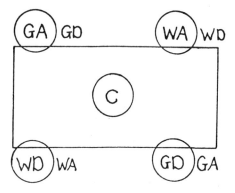

If the two end thirds of the court are used 20 children can work on this activity at any one time.

5. Landing and pivoting

Age range
Eight to nine.

Group size
Individuals and small teams.

What you need
Netball court, netballs, chalk.

What to do
An important rule in netball is that once a player has the ball she cannot move with it. This rule starts from as soon as the ball is in the child's hands. This means that the children need to learn about their landing foot or the foot which touches the ground first on catching the ball. This foot cannot be put back on the ground if it is lifted again, until the ball has been thrown. This means that the landing foot is best left on the ground unless the child is shooting. However, the children can step off from the landing foot and this way gain distance.

The non-landing foot can be moved and should act as a brake when the child first lands. However, it is the landing foot that counts when calculating the 1m rule.

To enable the children to practise landing properly they should initially become used to the idea that they have a foot which they can't move.

Teach the children to pivot, in other words, to turn around on the spot. To do this the child must find a part of the court where there are two or more lines crossing – you can draw more if necessary. She must then imagine that her landing foot is held by a magnet to the cross. She should use her other foot to 'paddle' round in a circle – this is pivoting. The child can turn in either direction, but at the end of the pivot, her landing foot should still be on the cross.

Ask the child to move away from the cross and then to run towards it, jump, and land with one foot on the cross. She should brake with her other foot and then pivot, taking care that she doesn't move her landing foot. Let her do this several times and then point out that usually people land on the same foot.

Ask the children to form pairs. One child in each pair should have a ball and stand about 1.5m away from the cross. The child without the ball should also stand away from the cross and to the side of her partner. The child with the ball should make a shoulder pass towards the circle and as she throws the ball the other player should run in, catch the ball, land and pivot ready to do a chest pass back to her partner. Make sure both the children have a chance to throw and catch the ball.

6. Small games

Age range
Eight to nine.

Group size
Individuals and small teams.

What you need
Bands or bibs.

What to do
Once the children understand the idea about landing feet, they can start to play small versions of netball using a third of the court. They can start with two against two and then three against three and they will need bibs and bands. When the children are capable of playing four against four and five against five they can play a game on the whole court. (This size game can also be played inside.)

When playing four against four the teams should be made up from two centres, one goalkeeper and one goal shooter. The centres are allowed to go anywhere on the court except the semi-circles. The goalkeeper is allowed in his own defending semi-circle and everywhere else, but not in the opposition's semi-circle. The goal shooter is allowed in

the attacking circle and everywhere else except the defending circle.

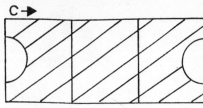

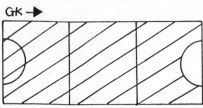

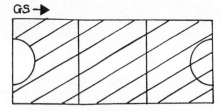

The ball can be thrown any distance except from one semi-circle to the other.

When playing with teams of five the positions used are: goalkeeper, goal defence, centre, goal attack, and goal shooter. The same rules for the four-sided game apply here and the goal defence and goal attack use the same areas as the goal keeper and goal shooter in the four-sided game.

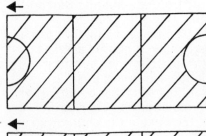

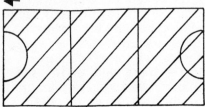

Make sure the children are all aware of their positions and functions before you let them start to play a game.

7. Positions and rules

Age range
Eight to nine.

Group size
Individuals and small teams.

What you need
Bands or bibs.

What to do
Below is shown all the positions used in a full game of netball and the areas of the court where they are allowed to play.

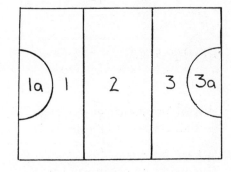

• The goalkeeper is allowed in areas 1a and 1.
• The goal defence is allowed in areas 1a, 1 and 2.
• The wing defence is allowed in areas 1 and 2.
• The centre is allowed in areas 1, 2 and 3.
• The wing attack is allowed in areas 2 and 3
• The goal attack is allowed in areas 2, 3 and 3a.
• The goal shooter is allowed in areas 3 and 3a.

All the players in the game are both defenders and attackers. However, each position does have the responsibility to mark certain other positions which are usually the people they stand next to at the start of the game. This is the job of every player when their team is in the defending position even though some children's individual position may be an attacking one.

The children should now be ready to play a proper game. They need to be briefed about the rules of the game, but this is best done as the need arises so that they get to know the rules in context. There are special rules for the primary school game and these are set out in the official rule book.

8. Improving the game

Age range
Eight to nine.

Group size
Individuals, pairs and small groups.

What you need
Netball courts, posts, netballs.

What to do
The exercises set out in this activity are ones which can be used at any stage, although they are really designed to improve the game. You should never be afraid of stopping the game and setting a practice for one particular aspect of it.

Speed/accuracy of passing/ catching
Ask the children to work in groups of eight using the whole width of the court. They should stand in groups of four at each side of the court. Place the ball in the middle of the court on the ground. The first child on one side of the court should run to the ball, pick it up, and use a chest pass to throw it to the first child on the other side of the court. He must then run to join the end of the line of the group opposite.

The child who has the ball should run and place it back in the middle of the court and join the end of the line of the other team. As she passes the new first child in this team they should tag hands and the new first child can run, pick up the ball and throw it.

At the end of the practice the children should all be standing on the opposite side of the court from where they started. This can be made more competitive by seeing which team finishes first.

Accuracy/throwing/catching one handed
Ask the children to start off by practising accuracy. They should work in pairs and start off by standing facing one another about 2m apart. One child should have the ball and the other should stand with his arms outstretched to either side, palms facing the child holding the ball. The child with the ball must then try to hit the hands of her partner with the ball. They can have ten throws each and see which of the pair has most hits.

If the children are proficient at catching with both hands this practice can be repeated with the child catching the ball one handed. The catching hand should 'give' on impact,

close around the ball and then gather it into the body. The thrower can send the ball to alternate hands, but as the children become better at the practice get the thrower to make random passes.

When the children are ready, they can practise passing the ball between themselves doing all the different types of passes that have been covered. The aim is to outwit their partner and make them drop the ball.

9. Skill practice: 1

Age range
Eight to nine.

Group size
Individuals, pairs and small groups.

What you need
Netball courts, posts, netballs.

What to do
Shooting practice
In this practice the children work in pairs. One child in the pair should stand with a ball, outside the circle but within the attacking third, while the other stands at the edge of the circle. The player with the ball shouts 'play' and then passes the ball using one of the passes previously covered. The other child must run to a position near the goalpost, receive the ball and take the shot. Each child can have five passes and shots and they can see who is the most accurate shot. You can also add defending players so that marking and dodging can also be practised.

Passing and shooting
Organise the children into groups of seven and tell them to stand at the goal-line at one end of the court. Specify which pass the children are to use and ask them to pass the ball to each other as they move down the court, but only using half of the width of the court. As they move down, the ball must be passed and received by all seven players. The team can only have a shot at the goal when one or more players are in the circle at the opposite end of the court to where they started. If the ball is dropped at any point, the children must start again.

There will be room to get two teams of seven on to one court at any one time if the teams start at opposite ends.

Once the children have practised this, the two groups can compete against each other to see which one scores most points in the given time.

Catching and pivoting practice
Tell the children to work in pairs using any line on the court. One child should stand on the line while the other throws the ball, using a shoulder pass, to either the right or the left of his partner. He must run to intercept the ball, and jump to catch it, landing, pivoting and throwing it back. He must then run back along the line, because as soon as the first child receives the ball, she will pass it in the direction of, but to one side of, him again.

Intercepting
The children can work in groups of four to seven. Ask one child to take the ball while the others stand in a group facing her. She must then throw the ball upwards using a shoulder pass, and the others must jump to try to catch the ball before anyone else. The one who successfully intercepts the ball is the next thrower.

10. Skill practice: 2

Age range
Eight to nine.

Group size
Individuals, pairs and small groups.

What you need
Netball courts, posts, netballs.

What to do
Intercepting/defending/ shooting
Use the practice activity on intercepting from the previous lesson, but this time split the children into two teams. (There will need to be at least five children in each team.) One team will act as the defending team while the other will be the attacking team. If an attacker catches the ball he scores a point for his team, and vice versa. The odd player is the thrower. Let the children change places so that the child who caught the ball becomes the thrower and the odd player who originally threw the ball joins one of the teams.

You can also make this into a shooting practice if you like. This time the odd player should stand outside the circle with the rest of the children inside. If an attacking player gets the ball she must shoot at goal and if she scores she gains a point. The defending team only have to intercept the ball to score a point. The attacking player may not pass, but must have a shot at goal from wherever she receives the ball in the circle. The defenders must move to positions to try to intercept the ball.

Remind the defenders that the interceptor needs to have her knees bent and be on her toes as she will need to jump upwards and towards the ball as the thrower starts to throw. The timing of the jump is essential so that the defender does not infringe the 1m rule.

Defending
Ask the children to stand side by side with a partner. One child is the defender and the other the attacker. On a given signal the attacker should start running, changing direction and speed. The defender also sets off, trying to stay as close as possible to her partner without making contact.

Speed/getting a loose ball
Tell the children to work in threes. They should start off by standing side by side and the child in the middle should hold the ball. He then rolls the ball along the ground in a straight line and as it rolls he counts to three. On 'three' the other two children must chase after the ball and pick it up. The child who gets the ball first becomes the new roller.

Throwing/catching/ pivoting
Working in groups of eight, ask two children to stand at each corner of a square.

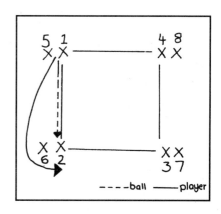

The child with the ball should throw it at the child opposite and then run after the ball to stand behind the other child waiting at this corner. The child who catches the ball should then pass it across and follow it and so on. This practice can carry on for as long as is needed. You can add restrictions, for example, if the ball is dropped the game has to start again. If there are several teams, the winning team could be the one to complete a full circuit first.

11. Skill practice: 3

Age range
Eight to nine.

Group size
Individuals, pairs and small groups.

What you need
Netball courts, posts, netballs, skittles.

What to do
The following practices can also be used as warm-ups before a team game.

The chest pass, pivoting and catching
Provide enough balls so that there is one for every two children. Mark out a 2m line using two markers or skittles. Give one child in the pair the ball and ask the other child to stand next to one of the two markers. The child with the ball should throw it to the unoccupied marker and the other child should run to catch the ball, land, pivot and throw the ball back to the first child. He should then catch the ball and throw it to the other marker and so on. Make sure that the children swap places after a few goes.

Footwork, the bounce pass, the chest pass and the shoulder pass
Ask the child to choose a partner and to stand about 1m away. The child who has the ball should throw it to his partner using a bounce pass. The receiver should then do the same back. He should then do a shoulder pass over his partner's head. She must run back to catch the ball, land, pivot and do a chest pass back.

She should then run back to her starting position ready to receive a bounce pass from her partner again. Repeat this a few times and then let the children swap places.

Passing, accuracy of passing and landings
Organise the children into groups of seven with one ball per group. The first child starts with the ball and passes it to the second child. This child runs towards the third child and throws the ball so

that it is caught by the first child about mid-way between her starting point and the third child. The first child should land after catching the ball and pass it to the third child. The first child then runs round the seventh child and the third child throws the ball to the second child and so on, until the children have all returned to their original positions. This practice will begin with very slow passes but gradually the children will begin to move the ball at top speed.

Second ball

Let the children play a game of netball but keep another ball with you. At any time during the game call out one of the children's names and throw the extra ball into play. The other ball must then be caught and thrown back to you by this child. The aim of this game is to help the teams to cope with a quick break from defence to attack and *vice versa*.

General game play

Inevitably, some players will be stronger than others. Avoid spreading the stronger players evenly between the two teams as they will just pass the ball between themselves. Split the strong players up so that the strong attack is marked by the strong defence. If the action is still one sided, try using the second ball idea.

Throw-ups

Practise specific things such as throw-ups. The children can work in threes with one ball. Give one child the ball while the other two players face each other, 1m apart, with their arms down by their sides. The child with the ball should do a waist-high throw-up and at the same time say 'play'. The two other children must try to grab the ball. Make sure the children do a total of nine throw-ups, three each, and see what each child scores.

Throw-ins

Ask the children to work in groups of six. Tell them to use the semi-circle and play a game of netball so that there are three children against three. Begin by giving one child the ball and asking her to stand behind the goal-line. She is marked using the 1m rule. She then says 'play' and this is the cue for the other players to move into either attacking or defending positions. The attacking team score if they shoot and get a goal and the defending team score if they intercept the ball and then make three consecutive passes.

Speed and accuracy under pressure

Ask the children to work in groups of seven with one ball per group. Ask them to form a circle with one child standing in the middle and one outside the circle. The children must then pass the ball around the circle using a chest pass and sending the ball back to the centre each time. The child on the outside must run around the circle and beat the ball. Having run around the circle, the child then rejoins the circle, swapping over with one of the children there. If the ball is dropped the children must start again.

This practice can also be played without using a child in the centre, but in this formation the children can pass the ball using a chest or bounce pass.

Hockey

Use the warm-ups provided at the beginning of this chapter before each hockey session. If hockey is being introduced into the school for the first time, there are a variety of sticks on the market including plastic ones. It might be a good idea to consult your PE adviser when choosing sizes and materials.

1. Dribbling

Age range
Nine to ten.

Group size
Individuals, pairs, and small groups.

What you need
Hockey sticks, hockey balls.

What to do
This lesson will be fairly static so it is important that the children do an active warm-up.

Before they learn how to dribble the ball the children will need to be taught the correct grip. It doesn't matter if the child is left- or right-handed as the grip is the same in both cases. The left hand is placed at the top of the stick and the right is placed about half way down (see diagram).

Tell the child to keep his feet together and the stick to the right of his feet. Check all the children's grips before they go any further.

When dribbling, the ball is kept in contact with the stick at all times. The child should

start off stationary with his hands and ball in the correct position. His left arm should be extended downwards and he should be slightly bent (see diagram).

The children can now start to move with the ball, but at first only at walking pace. Tell them to keep their balls slightly ahead and to the side of their front feet, but they should not allow the balls to lose contact with their sticks.

Once the children are competent at dribbling a ball at walking pace they should move progressively faster, making sure that their grip and stance remain in the correct position and that the ball does not leave the stick.

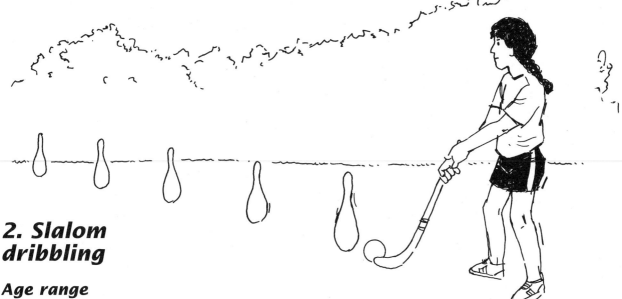

2. Slalom dribbling

Age range
Nine to ten.

Group size
Individuals and small groups.

What you need
A stick and ball per child, skittles.

What to do
Remind the children of the correct grip and basic skills for dribbling. Set out a line of five skittles, one for each group and tell the children that they should each dribble a ball, one at a time, around the skittles. They will need to be shown that they must move their feet so that the stick stays to their right all the time. It must also be impressed on them that they should not use the wrong side of the stick.

Once all the children have had a turn, you can introduce the idea that as well as watching the ball, they should also be aware of the other children around them. They can practise this awareness by dribbling a ball at walking pace in a small area. As they become more skilled they can increase their speed, trotting and then running. They must avoid touching anyone or anything and at the same time keep control of the ball by keeping it in contact with their stick. This practice should emphasise to the children the importance of keeping the ball close to their sticks and also of watching the others around them.

Play a small team game to help the children practise dribbling. Divide them into groups of five or six and tell each group to stand in a line with about 1m between each child. The child at the front of the line should then dribble his ball around the other children in their team and back to his original starting point. He should then dribble the ball in a straight line and pass it on to the next member of his team, remembering to keep the ball near his stick rather than 'pushing' it to the next child. He must then return to his starting position. The child who now has the ball should dribble around the team, taking care that she goes round the first child. Every child must have a go and the game finishes when the last child in the line has had his turn.

3. The push

Age range
Nine to ten.

Group size
Individuals and pairs.

What you need
Hockey sticks, hockey balls, skittles.

What to do
Once the children have gained some degree of stick/ball co-ordination they can move on to look at the push. This skill is the one which starts the game of hockey and the grip is the same as for dribbling. The ball is positioned to the right of the child's left foot and to the front of it. The child's right foot is placed behind her body so that her weight is spread and her centre of gravity is lowered. She then places her stick behind the ball so that it touches it.

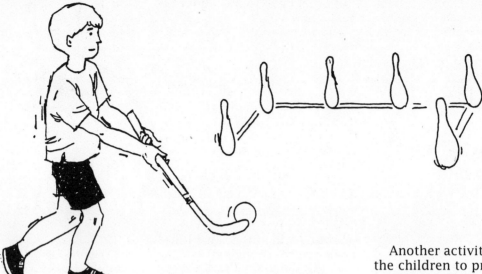

She should look at the ball at all times during the push and she must not take her stick away from the ball. By slightly pulling back her left hand and pushing with her right hand she should push the ball forwards. At the same time she should bring her weight forward. There should be no lifting of the ball; if the ball does go off the ground it is because the face of the stick was not kept square to the ball, or the child was looking up when the ball was pushed.

Let the children start off by pushing a stationary ball. Once they have mastered the technique, introduce the idea of accuracy by placing two skittles as mini-goals. The children can then try and push their balls through. The skittles need only be a short distance away from the children to begin with, but you should increase the distance as they become more proficient.

As the children become adept, introduce the idea of pushing a moving ball. To do this, the child should dribble the ball and then spread her feet into the correct position to push it. If she needs to push in another direction she should move her feet into the correct position rather than using her wrists to initiate the change of direction.

Let the children practise their pushing skills in pairs, sending the ball backwards and forwards between each other.

Another activity enabling the children to practise their pushing skills is shooting. The children can stand around the semi-circle and dribble the ball towards the goal. After about 2m they should push the ball and try to score a goal.

4. Stopping the ball

Age range
Nine to ten.

Group size
Individuals, pairs and small groups.

What you need
Hockey sticks, hockey balls.

What to do
Once the children have got the ball moving they need to be taught how to stop it. Again the grip is the same as for dribbling. The child should hold his stick in front of his feet and keep it straight. He should be able to look at an imaginary wrist-watch on his left wrist. His left hand should

be further away from his body than his right so that the stick is at a right angle. This stops the ball from travelling up the stick (see diagram).

The angled stick also traps the ball and therefore stops it bouncing away from the stick. Point out that if the ball bounces away from the stick an opponent may get it. As the ball hits the stick the child's right hand should 'give' a little to absorb the impact of the ball. It should be stressed that the child's feet must be kept behind the stick when stopping the ball which means that he will have to move his feet to get into the correct position. It should also be stressed that the ball won't always reach the player and he will often have to go and meet it.

Once the children have mastered the correct positioning they should work in pairs pushing and stopping the ball between them. If time permits they should form into threes where one child pushes to another, who stops the ball, moves his feet and pushes to the last child.

As the children move down the field the push should be in a diagonal direction, into the pathway of the next child to receive the ball. Once all three children have received the ball they should pass it back the opposite way until they reach the end of the field.

This practice can also be used later on along with dribbling and hitting. Shooting can also be added, with the children doing a push shot at a skittle goal at the end of the field.

5. Push hockey

Age range
Nine to ten.

Group size
Groups of three.

What you need
Hockey sticks, hockey balls, skittles, bibs or bands.

What to do
Tell the children that they are going to play a pushing game. The rules are that the children are allowed to push the ball, but are not allowed to dribble or tackle. To gain possession of the ball they must intercept it. This will introduce the idea of marking where the children must be positioned between the ball and the player they are marking.

Use skittles to mark the goal. Each team should have a

goalkeeper (changed at regular intervals to avoid her getting cold) and the game starts with a push back, with the child taking the push facing her own goal. Everyone else must be 'on-side', standing in their own halves.

Once the game starts, the children are allowed to go anywhere on the pitch, pushing the ball to their own team while the opposing team try to intercept and gain possession.

6. Hitting the ball

Age range
Nine to ten.

Group size
Individuals, pairs and small groups.

What you need
Hockey sticks, hockey balls, skittles.

What to do
In this lesson the children will learn how to hit a ball. The grip used to do this is different from the one used previously and this provides the starting point. The child's left hand is kept at the top of the stick and her right hand is positioned just below it so that her little finger of her right hand is touching the index finger of her left. The child should stand sideways on to the ball which is placed level with her front foot. Her left foot is positioned behind and to the side of her right foot.

Having learned the grip, children can move on to hitting the ball. Each child should start with her stick behind the ball and then take it backwards. There is no rule to say how high a stick can be lifted, but there is a rule about dangerous play, so the children need to be taught that the stick should not be swung wildly. The child should bend her arms as she swings backwards and this should limit any possible wildness. As the stick swings through, the child should hit the ball square

on. If the stick doesn't make square contact with the ball the child may have dropped her right shoulder or she may have brought the stick down instead of swinging through. If she is doing either of these she should practise 'cutting the grass', where she has to brush the top of the grass without leaving any divets.

If the child is hitting the top of the ball instead of square on, she may need to adjust the position of her feet. It is always worth checking the position of the children's feet before looking for other problems.

The stick should follow through once the ball has been struck. The end of the swing should find the child with her stick pointing at where she wanted the ball to go to. Her wrists should be kept firm but not stiff and this is the case throughout the swing. The firmness of her wrists in the follow-through will stop the stick being wrapped around the child's legs at the end of the swing! The child must keep her head 'over' the ball to prevent it going upwards into the air. This action also means that she will keep her eye on the ball throughout the hitting process.

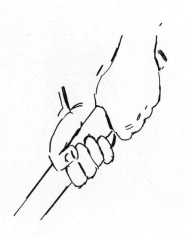

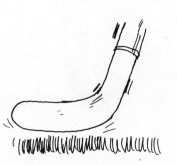

Once the children have grasped the idea they should join with a partner and practise hitting and stopping. They will need to be reminded how to stop the ball and it should be stressed to them that they must meet the ball and have their feet behind the stick. The children can then progress to dribbling and hitting the ball. They will need to change their grip from the dribbling position to the hitting position and to do this they must slide their right hands up the stick as they turn sideways to get their feet into the correct hitting position.

Once they have mastered the change of grip they can practise hitting and dribbling. In order to do this they should dribble a short distance and then hit the ball. They can use a skittle as a marker to show where the hit must take place. The children must then follow their ball and dribble it to the end of the field.

You may also want to include shooting practice and if so this may be added at the end of the session.

Further activities
• Ask the children to dribble the ball towards a goal and shoot once they reach a skittle placed about 3m away from the goal.
• Ask the children to stand on a line and do a stationary hit and then run after their balls. See who can hit the ball the farthest.
• Repeat the practice for dribbling and pushing but ask the children to hit the ball instead of pushing it.

7. Consolidating skills

Age group
Nine to ten.

Group size
Individuals and pairs.

What you need
Sticks, balls, skittles.

What to do
The aim of this lesson is to give the children time to practise and consolidate the skills they have learned so far.

• Ask the children to shoot at a goal (skittles may be used) from different angles. They should use a standing push or a standing hit. Tell the children to stand about 3m from the goal.
• Let the children repeat the practice they did earlier involving pushing and hitting the ball across the field in threes.
• Ask the children to dribble a ball around a line of skittles. The children should dribble to one end of the skittles and then wait for the rest of their group to do the same. When one child is about half way down the row of skittles, the next one can set off. Try to make the groups as small as possible, although this will be dependent on the number of skittles available.

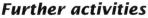

8. Tackling and dodging

Age range
Nine to ten.

Group size
Pairs and small groups.

What you need
Hockey sticks, hockey balls, skittles, bibs or bands.

What to do
The children should work in pairs with one ball between them. One child should act as the tackler, while the other is the player who has the ball. There are two ways of tackling.

The first is the up and over tackle where the ball is trapped between the two sticks and the tackler pulls the ball upwards and over his opponent's stick by pushing hard at the ball and pulling upwards at the same time. The grip is as for dribbling.

The second is the pull-away tackle where the tackler drags the ball toward the left of her opponent, remembering to move her feet so that the ball does not hit him. The tackler then continues to dribble and the child who has been robbed will want to give chase to try and regain possession; he runs around the player with the ball to avoid obstructing her. (As a general rule you should tell the children that the way to avoid obstructing, or 'turning' as it is called in some situations, is to make sure that they never have their backs to their opponents.) In this particular tackling technique the children should always make sure that they tackle the ball and not the stick. The dribbling grip is used.

The two tackles should be introduced separately. The children should practise each tackle, with the child who is being tackled initially standing still and making no effort to tackle back.

The children then need to be told about dodging. Point out to them that there is only one sure way of keeping possession of the ball and that is by doing an accurate pass before their opponent gets too near. However, this will not always be possible, so the children need to know what else they can do. Explain to them that as their opponent approaches they can push the ball to the non-stick side of him and then run round him to collect the ball. Remind the children that they must run round to avoid obstructing or turning.

Ask the children to work in pairs. The child who is the opponent should stand still and let her partner make several attempts at dodging. (Progression in this practice is achieved by the opponent moving towards the ball.) There are other dodges, but these require skills which have not yet been covered.

Once the children have grasped the basic idea of tackling and dodging they can play a small game in teams of two on a limited area of the pitch. The children can decide which line or skittle they are 'shooting' at and they should score a point every time they get the ball over the line or past the skittle. The pairs should work as a team in which each of them have the responsibility for marking or tackling one of the opposing two children. Remind them that even if they don't have the ball, their opponent should be marked by them standing between the ball and the player.

Further activity
Increase the number of children in each team by putting two groups together. Of course, the playing area will also need to be expanded and you may decide to restrict the shots used to push passes only.

A further progression could be to play using teams of eight. This would entail some further explanation about positioning, since with teams this big the children would need to spread out rather than cluster around the ball.

9. Indoor hockey

Age group
Nine to ten.

Group size
Groups of four or fives.

What you need
Indoor sticks, a quoit or puck, bibs or bands.

What to do
The disadvantage of the indoor game is that, because of the limited numbers of children that can play at one time, there tends to be quite a lot of children sitting out at any one time. However, you can swap the teams in and out of the game regularly to avoid the children getting bored.

One big difference between the indoor and outdoor versions of the game is that the children can use both sides of the indoor stick. The sticks are usually plastic, but wooden sticks can be used if a sock is put over the head to avoid scratching polished floors. The rules of the game are as follows:
• The game begins with a push-back as in the outdoor version.
• There is no hitting and only push passes are allowed; this means that the children may not lift their sticks backwards. This is a safety aspect as the children will be playing in a fairly small area and a back lift could be dangerous. The ball is not allowed to go into the air for the same reason.
• The goalkeepers are the only players who are allowed into the semi-circles and they should use their sticks to stop shots at goal and they can lay them flat to the ground in order to do this. If any other player goes into the semi-

circle, whether they are defenders or attackers, the other team is given a penalty push. It is taken from the edge of the semi-circle.
• The other members of the team are allowed to go anywhere on the pitch except in the semi-circles.
• A goal may be scored from anywhere, but it must be pushed from outside the semi-circle.
• The ball does not go out of play since the walls or upturned benches are counted as part of the pitch.
• If a child kicks the ball, barges, lifts the ball or their stick, then a free push is given to the opposing team.

Having explained the basic rules, let the children play the game in teams of four or five.

NB: It is advisable for the children to wear some kind of footwear when playing indoor hockey.

Cricket

Before teaching specific cricket skills it is a good idea to use a number of sessions to revise throwing and catching skills.

1. Fielding

Age range
Ten to eleven.

Group size
Individuals and pairs.

What you need
Small balls.

What to do
Revise the technique of catching a ball, always using a soft ball. The children should try to judge the flight of a ball as it is thrown into the air and place their bodies in its line of flight. Remind them to spread their fingers and bring the ball in towards their bodies.

Put the children into pairs, with one child throwing and the other catching. At first the children should stand very close together, throwing the ball gently. As they grow more proficient move them farther apart.

After a time, move the children on to fielding and stopping the ball. The children should move into the path of a ball thrown along the ground. They should place their hands in a cupped position in front of the ball and 'give' as the ball enters their hands. They should try to place their whole bodies behind the ball in case of a misfield.

Put the children back into pairs, so that one child throws the ball and the other fields it and throws it back.

2. The under-arm cricket throw

Age range
Ten to eleven.

Group size
Individuals and pairs.

What you need
Small balls.

What to do
Warm-up with the children throwing balls to each other and retrieving them. Then teach and demonstrate the under-arm throw. To do this correctly the child should grip the ball with his fingers, step forward on to his left foot, bringing his right foot up behind. He should swing his right arm back (reverse the motions for left-handed players) and step forward with his left foot and at the same time swing his right arm forward, releasing the ball.

Let the children practise delivering the ball in this manner, aiming at a mark on the wall set at a height roughly equivalent to the delivery point of the ball at the batsman. Then move the children into pairs and let them practise throwing the ball to one another.

3. The over-arm cricket throw

Age range
Ten to eleven.

Group size
Individuals and pairs.

What you need
Small soft balls.

What to do
Teach and demonstrate the technique of the over-arm throw. The child should grip the ball with her fingers and stand sideways. Her non-throwing arm and shoulder should be pointed at the target and her throwing arm should be brought back behind her body as she transfers her weight from her front to her back foot. She should then whip her throwing arm through and at the same time transfer her weight back on to her front foot. She should rotate her body as her arm comes forward and use the force of her knees, hips, trunk and shoulders to give power to her throwing arm.

Once the children have practised this technique, ask them to throw their balls at a target. They should follow through across the front of their bodies to the opposite side.

Give each child three or four balls and allow the class to practise this technique, throwing the balls and running after them. After a sufficient interval, put the children into pairs and tell them to throw the balls to one another, slowly increasing the distance between them.

4. The cricket bowling action

Age range
Ten to eleven.

Group size
Individuals and pairs.

What you need
Small soft balls.

What to do
Most schools adopt versions of cricket which involve an under-arm bowling action, but it might be worth introducing the over-arm bowling action, even if only a few children are able to grasp the technique. They can then practise the skill in small groups.

To bowl properly the child should grip the ball and adopt a controlled run-up, so that her feet straddle the bowling line at the moment of delivery. As the ball is bowled, she should turn her right foot sideways and lean away from the batsman, with her back arched and her weight back. She should extend her left arm upwards and bring over her bowling arm to face the front, transferring her weight to her front foot. She should keep her bowling arm straight and release the ball from as high a point as possible making sure that her arm follows through to cross to the other side of her body.

Allow the children to practise this movement, supervising and helping them. The most difficult part of the action lies in keeping the bowling arm straight at the moment of delivery.

If the children seem to grasp the technique then let them bowl at one another in pairs. Do not be disappointed if only a few of the children show any signs of developing the correct technique, but persevere with these few children in subsequent group activities.

5. The batting stance

Age range
Ten to eleven.

Group size
Individuals and pairs.

What you need
Cricket bats, small soft balls.

What to do
Make sure that the bats which the children are using are not too big or too heavy for them. Demonstrate the correct hold; if a right-handed player, the child should place his hands together with his left hand near to the top of the handle. He should place his left hand so that the back of it faces down the pitch slightly, diagonally away from the body. He should grip his fingers and thumbs round the handle, lining up the two 'Vs' formed by his index finger and thumb of each hand. Tell him to stand sideways with his feet slightly apart and roughly parallel. He should incline the bat slightly inwards, resting the handle against the upper leg. Stress the importance of keeping his head up and facing the bowler.

Supervise the children as they adopt this stance, giving them help when required. Make sure that their body weight is evenly distributed. When the stance has been mastered by most of the children, demonstrate the basic forward stroke.

To do this stroke the child should place his front foot as close to the pitch and line of the ball as possible, bending his knee to allow his body weight to come forward. Tell him to use his upper arm and wrist to control the stroke, keeping his elbow high. He should hit the ball using the full face of the bat, pushing through it if the stroke is to be an attacking one.

Organise the children into pairs, and ask one child to lob a ball to the other. The batter should adopt the correct stance and then go forward into the stroke.

NB: Always use soft balls in any cricket practice.

6. Non-stop cricket

Age range
Ten to eleven.

Group size
Small groups.

What you need
Cricket bats, small balls, stumps.

What to do
Once the children have warmed-up they can move on to play a game of cricket. The size of the teams can vary from as few as eight players to as many as twenty. Place three stumps at the end of the pitch and another stump about 10m away for the bowler to bowl from. Finally, place another stump about 8m to the right of the three stumps.

Decide which team will be batting and which bowling and let the bowling side distribute its fielders. The first child to bowl must then bowl the ball at the batter who should stand by the three stumps, and the batter must attempt to strike the ball. Even if the batter does not make contact she must run towards the stump to the right of her and back to the three stumps. The ball meanwhile must be returned to the bowler by the fielders and she can bowl again immediately. If the stumps are knocked down the batter is out and the next batter takes over.

7. Tower ball

Age range
Ten to eleven.

Group size
Groups of five.

What you need
Skittles, chalk, large balls.

What to do
Mark out two large circles on the ground – one inside the other. In the centre of the smaller circle place a skittle. Tell one team to stand on the edge of the larger circle while the second team stand around the inner circle. The first team must try to knock down the skittle by throwing or rolling the ball in a variety of ways. The second team has to try to defend the skittle with their arms, legs and bodies. Once the first team has knocked down the skittle three times the teams change places.

CHAPTER 4

Gymnastic activities

The National Curriculum requires that primary children are able to do the following at Key Stage 1:

• travel;
• turn;
• roll;
• jump;
• balance;
• swing;
• climb;
• take weight on their hands.

All these activities should be experienced on both the floor and apparatus and the children should be given the opportunity to practise, adapt and improve their control of individual actions leading up to making up their own sequences.

At Key Stage 2 the requirements are the same, but children should be working on each in greater depth while also looking at speed, direction and body shape. By Key Stage 2, their sequence work should show how one action can lead into the next.

Finally, at both key stages, the children need to be taught how to get out and put away the apparatus, including safe lifting techniques.

The aim of this chapter is to provide the primary school teacher with activities which she can use to develop her own experience and that of the children in the area of gymnastics. The intention is to provide themes which can be explored and developed according to the response of the children and the level of their skill through activities.

BACKGROUND

Themes

The themes in this chapter are used as vehicles to deliver action words. For example, if locomotion is the theme the action words rolling and jumping will be included in it.

Finally, at the end of each theme, an action phrase is introduced which the children can use to make a movement sequence.

Cohesion and progression may be added to a gymnastics programme by selecting a main theme for each year, involving basic actions. This is not essential, but for those teachers wishing to adopt this whole school approach the following themes are suggested:
• locomotion –travelling, jumping, rolling;
• balance – large/small bases, stability/instability, symmetry/asymmetry;
• twist and turn – all the previous themes, but with emphasis on direction and body shape;
• tip, twist, jump, roll, fall and swing – builds on previous themes, but adds the concept of initiating and concluding movement using these action words;
• contract and stretch – body shape and levels;
• flight – takes the previously explored action word 'jump' further;
• partner work – takes the idea of partner work to more complex levels such as using a partner as an obstacle and counter-tension/counter-balance.

Running through all the above main themes are the sub-themes of level, direction, speed and body shape.

Educational gymnastics should make children think about what their bodies are doing and how they are doing it. They should be taught to respond to the challenges you set them and to produce their best work at all times. Specific skills can be introduced along the way. Although the children should bring out many of the ideas used, teacher direction is also necessary in order to introduce new ideas to the class through various movements.

A theme will take several weeks to work through, especially if specific skills are to be taught. However, once a theme has been completed an action phrase can then be introduced. An action phrase is usually in the form of a number of actions, such as travel, jump, roll, which have been explored through the theme. This action phrase should be used to produce the sequence which the children work on and eventually perform. Throughout this sequence the quality of performance should be stressed; the sequence itself must be the best work that the children can produce whether they are budding gymnasts or struggling to do even the most basic actions.

An action phrase is designed to take at least two weeks working at floor level, two weeks on low apparatus such as benches, low box tops and mats and a further two weeks on larger apparatus. If it is decided to allow the children to show their work (usually a worthwhile exercise), then another week needs to be added to each phase of the work for this final programme.

Whatever the children are doing, praise is essential, whether they have just mastered the bunny hop or performed some complicated movement. Any assessment should be of an individual nature and not by judging the rest against the best.

Children should in time cover all aspects of educational gymnastics, but you should take care not to introduce a new theme if the children are still struggling with an earlier one. This also applies when the children move to a new class.

Each activity in this chapter is not necessarily intended to be covered in one lesson. Take time to explore the particular activity; the allocations here are only suggestions. If the children are interested and still coming up with fresh ideas then stay with the activity!

Practical hints

It is important that during a gymnastics lesson, you are in charge of all aspects of the lesson, both to enhance the learning process and to cover all safety precautions. If the children learn the basic rules while doing floorwork this will enable you to remain in control of the situation more easily when the children are scaling large apparatus.

There are two basic rules that are necessary for safety.
• The children must always stop when they are told to. (If on apparatus the children should stop where they are until they are told to climb down or carry on.)

• The children must maintain an acceptable level of noise so that they can hear you at all times.

If the children are working on an activity, they should be stopped every five minutes or so for you to point out good ideas or to remind them of some aspect that they are not covering properly. This routine helps to establish teacher control and ensures that the two rules are followed.

When talking to the children initially, ask them to sit down – this ensures teacher control. It is always helpful if you are able to demonstrate part of the work, but the demonstration should be reasonably sound technically. It is not a good idea to introduce your mistakes to the children! There are plenty of willing volunteers among the class should any be required!

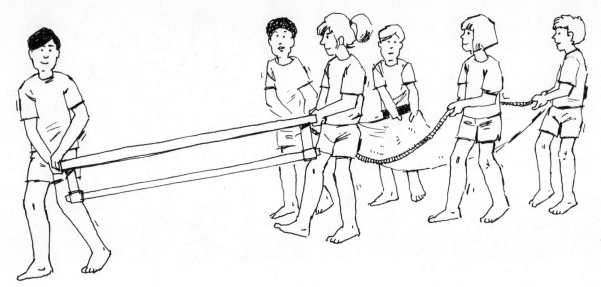

Clothing

The children should always change for gymnastics lessons. They should have bare feet unless, of course, they have a verruca. Jewellery should not be allowed on the grounds of safety (including earrings). Long hair should be tied back. All these are very important safety precautions.

Apparatus

All children should be taught to get out and put away the apparatus to be used. You may need a complete lesson if the children are being shown how to get out the larger apparatus. However, if you do devote a whole lesson to this, try to let the children do something on the apparatus before it is all put away again. If you try to make this activity 'fun', the children will feel that getting out the apparatus was worthwhile. An ideal activity to use is 'knockout words'. In this game the children start off standing in a clear space in the middle of the room. You should shout out a word of instruction, like 'brick', 'off the floor', 'partner', 'wood', 'metal' and so on. The last child to touch the appropriate object or perform the required action is out. Once a child is out she can help you to spot the next laggard, until only one child is left.

Setting up the apparatus should be done as a class activity. The first time the children get out larger apparatus you should show them how to set out one particular piece at a time and emphasise the safety checks involved. It is essential no child is allowed on any piece of apparatus until you have checked it.

When only using mats the children need to be told and shown the correct lifting technique, that is their knees must be bent and their thighs should take the strain of lifting and not the back. There should always be at least two children per mat. A good tip for getting out mats is for the children to play 'aeroplane'. They should all line up in two columns, either side and to the back of the mats. They should then pretend to follow the runway and pick up a mat on the way past. This avoids children getting trampled. To put the mats away simply reverse the process.

Apparatus should be put out in a set order each time:
• fixed apparatus, but not the ropes – they are liable to swing or be swung on;
• large portable apparatus;
• benches;
• mats;
• any other small pieces of equipment;
• ropes.

Obviously the age of the children involved will be a determining factor in what pieces may be set up, but even the youngest children can be taught to get out mats and benches.

After the children have been shown what to do, groups may be allocated to get out various pieces of apparatus. After it has all been set up the children should be given several warm-up activities so that they do not get cold, and also to bring them back to a gymnastic frame of mind!

For floorwork mats will be the only apparatus necessary, if they are needed at all. For intermediate or low apparatus benches or low box tops and mats may be needed. The progression of the activities is from floor, to low apparatus, to larger apparatus. The children should be given the opportunity to produce work using the various themes and the associated activities at all three levels of apparatus.

Warm-up activities

The children should always do a short warm-up before starting the lesson. This is not only essential to prevent injury, but it provides a good starting point for teacher control. If the body is not warmed-up properly, strains and pulled muscles may be the result. An added bonus is that the children seem to enjoy this routine!

Stretching exercises are good warm-up exercises as they encourage flexibility.

However, when a child stretches he should only go as far as is comfortable; the stretch should never be painful. When the optimum level of performance has been reached it should be held for a count of seven.

The warm-up itself should not last for too long – no longer than five minutes in a 20 minute session (not including changing time). The general warm-up below works all the parts of the body and can be done in about five minutes. However, when using it try to be selective and choose those areas most appropriate to the activity which is being covered in the lesson.

Neck
• Ask the child to lean her head to one side and then to the other, trying to touch her shoulder with her ear, without moving her shoulders. She should repeat this three times on each side.
• Ask the child to look from side to side with his chin on his chest and keeping his head down (in other words, looking at the floor). He should repeat this three times.

Arms
Ask the child to hold her arms straight out to each side of her body and wiggle her fingers. She should then circle her wrists in both directions – about three times each way. Tell the child to make circles with her lower arms around the elbow joint as if they were propellers. The child should then straighten her arms and make little circles using the whole arm, so that the shoulder joint moves. Finally, with her arms extended upwards, she should make circles forward and backward. For all these arm exercises repeat three times in each direction.

Waist/trunk
Ask the child to place his hands on his hips and position his feet so that they are shoulder-width apart. He should then bend three times on each side, so that he stretches his waist. Leaning forward and keeping his head

up, the child should make a big circle going round the side, to the back, to the side and then back to the front. Tell the child to repeat in the opposite direction.

Feet
Ask the child to keep her feet together and go up on to her toes. She should try to stretch as high as she can. In order to emphasise the movement the child should start from a slightly slouched position. Ask her to repeat this three times.

Legs and feet
Ask the child to sit down and put his legs together so that they are straight out in front of him. (Emphasise the need for good posture and a nice straight back.) Then tell the child to flex his feet by pulling his toes back towards his

knees until his leg muscles feel taut. Using only one leg at a time, he should lift his leg about 15cm (6in) off the floor and hold it for a count of seven. Ask him to repeat this twice with each leg.

Back and legs
Ask the child to stand up straight with her legs together and slightly bent, then ask her to curl back downwards. (Don't let her bend straight over as this may harm her back.) The child should go down as far as she can and hold her position for a count of seven. The aim is to get the palms flat on to the floor, always remembering to keep the legs slightly bent. Slowly uncurl, and then repeat one more.

Stomach
Ask the child to lie flat on the floor with his knees bent and his hands behind his head. (The hands are there as a support only and should not

be used to haul his head up.) Tell him to keep his eyes on the ceiling and then to gently push his chest and shoulders towards his thighs. Encourage him to hold this position for a count of seven and then relax. The child should repeat this twice. Make sure that he does not put his chin on his chest. The aim is not to sit up but rather to work the stomach muscles. If the child is doing this properly his stomach will feel hard.

Cool-down

At the end of each gymnastic lesson there should be at least two minutes allowed for a period of cool-down. These exercises should be gentle, encouraging the children to slow their bodies down and thus enable them to go back to the classroom in a calm manner. The back and leg exercises from the warm-up section are the type of activity which can be used to this effect.

ACTIVITIES

Locomotion

1. An introduction to travel

Age range
Four to five.

Group size
Individuals.

What you need
No special requirements.

What to do
Before you start this activity insist that the children are quiet. This is essential if they are not to regard the lesson as a playtime. You should establish this basic rule right from the start. It is important that the children hear any commands. Try to keep your voice fairly quiet so that the children actually have to listen.

Ask the children to walk around the room without touching anyone else. They should travel in a forward direction. After a while, tell them to change direction using the word 'turn'. The children will turn 90° on this command but they will still be walking forwards. Tell the children to change direction in this way two or three times. Then repeat the command but ask them to walk backwards. (They should be reminded that unless they have eyes in the back of their heads they will need to look over their shoulders to see where they are going.) They can then do the same but walking sideways.

Now introduce the children to the concept of levels. Ask them to walk at as low a level as they can maintain while remaining on their feet. Next they should walk like giants. To reinforce the idea of direction at the same time, use commands such as 'backwards-high' and 'forwards-low'.

Also bring in the idea of variations of speed, starting with fast and then going on to slow. Develop this with instructions like 'forward, high, fast' and so on.

Further activity
Introduce the idea of stopping slowly or suddenly. Incorporate a game of 'musical statues' into the activity.

2. Travelling on different parts of the body

Age range
Four to five.

Group size
Individuals.

What you need
Mats.

What to do
Ask the children to experiment with travelling on different parts of their bodies. They can use any body part except their feet. They could try:
• sliding on their fronts using only their hands to help them

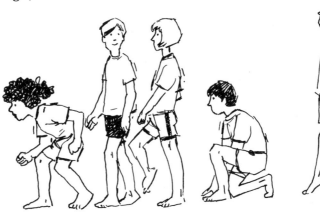

move, or commando style, using their elbows;

• walking on their bottoms, keeping their legs straight, lifting their hips, pushing forwards and using their arms to help;

• lying on their backs, curling up so that their knees are hugged to their chests and then rocking backwards and forwards;

• sitting with their legs apart and rolling from their sides to their backs to their sides again ending up facing in the opposite direction;

• walking on their hands (mats are essential) by putting their hands down, kicking their legs up and moving their hands forward;

• rolling (mats are essential) using a 'sausage' roll where the children lie full length on the floor with their arms above their heads. They should keep their legs straight and then roll sideways.

If the children are to attempt a forward roll they will first have to be taught the right way to do one and then be properly supervised to ensure that they are working safely and correctly. To do a forward roll properly the child should stand so that her feet are on the edge of the mat. She should crouch down so that her bottom is on her heels. She should then lean forward, extending her arms and placing her hands on the mat – shoulder-width apart and fingers and thumbs pointing forwards. At the same time she should push her bottom into the air, so that her legs are fairly straight, and then look at her knees and push forwards on to her toes so that they tip forwards. The child should make sure that she keeps her hands still so that the back of her neck touches the mat first. She should keep her legs in a tucked position as she rolls and try to stand after the roll by imagining that she is reaching forwards and pulling on a bar at the end of the mat.

Once the children have mastered the crouched start to the roll they should be taught how to begin a roll from a standing position. Instead of crouching, the children can stand with their feet touching the edge of the mat and their arms raised above their heads. They can then bend down into the crouched position and continue as before. The movement should not be stilted, but is a smooth transition from standing to rolling.

The point of teaching the crouch starting position first is so that the children will realise the importance of getting the back of their necks down straight away.

Further activity
Introduce the idea of levels when travelling on different parts of the body.

NB: Some children with certain special needs such as children with Downs' Syndrome must not attempt forward rolls as they can damage their necks.

3. The five basic jumps

Age range
Four to five.

Group size
Individuals.

What you need
Mats.

What to do
The five basic jumps are:
• one foot to the same foot (hop);

• one foot to the other foot (step);
• one foot to two feet;
• two feet to one foot;
• two feet to two feet.

Ask the children to practise jumping. They should work on the spot and you can point out to them the type of jump they are doing.

It is very important that the children are taught how to land correctly. They should 'give' at the ankles and knees so that the impact of the landing is absorbed through their legs. They should never land flat-footed as this will damage their backs.

Include all five jumps, asking each child to do them all. You should then ask the children to jump across a mat using one of the jumps and introduce the idea of body shape. The children can help to point out the different shapes each child makes as he jumps. Pick out interesting and different examples and let these children demonstrate them again. If one of the children hasn't already done one, introduce a star shape. Ask the children to show a two foot to two foot jump and make a spread out shape in the air. There are lots of other shapes which can be made. See how many the children can do.

Further activity
Explore direction and speed. For example, can the children take off in one direction, but land facing the way they came from? Can they do a slow, long jump or a fast, quick jump?

4. Travelling on hands and feet

Age range
Four to five.

Group size
Individuals.

What you need
Mats.

What to do
Take the opportunity to teach the children how to get into a crab position. (They may feel more at ease if they do the crab on a mat.) Start off by asking the children to move forwards on:
• two hands and two feet (tummy down);
• two hands and one foot;
• one hand and two feet;
• one hand and one foot.

Next ask the children to try a bunny hop using two hands and two feet. They should place their hands down on the floor and jump to the side of their hands.

Suggest they try a catspring, using two hands and two feet. They should put their hands out in front and jump their bottoms towards them so that their feet are brought forwards to, or even through, their hands.

Let the children try all the combinations of jumping using their hands and feet, but make sure that they all attempt a catspring and a bunny hop.

The children will now be ready to try to get into the crab position. If at all possible, provide a good demonstration of what this position looks like. To form a crab the child should lie on his back on the floor with his hands under his shoulders and his palms on the floor – fingers pointing

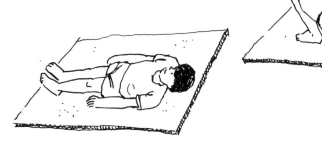

towards his feet. He should place his heels near to his bottom with his feet shoulder-width apart. Then he should push upwards with his hands and feet at the same time.

If the children can only raise up so that their heads are still touching the floor then this is fine, but they can continue to practise the position. Once they have mastered the basic technique the children should try walking, remembering that real crabs walk sideways!

Further activity
As most of the movements in this activity will have been at a low level, the children will need to be reminded that there are two other levels at which they can work. Use this opportunity to recap the five basic jumps where landing takes the child into a form of travel using hands and feet together.

5. Linking movement

Age range
Four to five.

Group size
Individuals.

What you need
Mats.

What to do
The aim of this lesson is to introduce the idea that movements can be linked together to form a sequence. To do this the children will need to use an action phrase; that is a series of action words which when put together form a phrase or sequence. In this case the *action phrase* is 'travel, jump, roll'. As this is the first time the children will have actually worked on an action phrase it is a good idea

to begin by giving them a simple example to copy. This should include actions with which the children are already familiar, for example:
• Travel – the children should slide on the floor on their fronts with their legs together, using their hands to pull themselves along towards a mat. They should do this five times and then, when they reach the mat, do a catspring into a standing position.
• Jump – from the standing position the children should do a two feet to two feet jump making a star shape in air. Remind them to land properly.
• Roll – the children should do a forward roll from the standing position they achieved in the jump. They should aim to finish the forward roll in a standing position.

Once the children have practised each part of the phrase separately, they can put them together to make one continual sequence with each action leading into the next. Stress to them that they must capture a feeling of stillness at

the beginning and end of their sequence so that their audience know when they are about to start and when they have finished.

Now let the children show their work to each other. They will probably all want to perform rather than watch someone else's work and so it is a good idea to split the class in half so that one half shows their work while the other half watches and then let the groups swap over.

Lay down some ground rules for when the children watch. They need to be made aware that it is expected that they will sit quietly and watch the other children work and that they should respond positively to what they see. It will also need to be made clear that their sequences have a beginning and ending and that the children should stick to these when demonstrating their work. If this isn't stressed from the outset some of the sequences may seem to last forever!

Further activity
If there is time, the children could go on to make up their own sequences using their own ideas for the action phrase of 'Travel, jump, roll'.

6. Making up a sequence

Age range
Four to five.

Group size
Individuals.

What you need
Mats.

What to do
In this activity the children will have the opportunity to make up their own sequences. Ensure that the children know what the action words are – 'travel, jump, roll'. Impress on them that their actions must be linked together. This will probably not happen straightaway, but keep reminding them. The children should be given time to develop their ideas and then be reminded about using different levels, directions and speed, although not all at the same time.

Make sure that there is no queuing for mats, by pointing out that the floor is also part of the work space. If you see a good idea or a good linked piece of work, ask the child to demonstrate it to the other children.

If there is time towards the end of the lesson the children should show their work to the rest of the class. They should be rewarded with, for example, applause or a positive comment.

7. Working with intermediate apparatus

Age range
Four to five.

Group size
Individuals.

What you need
Benches, mats.

What to do
Set out the apparatus, taking care that the children are shown the correct way to carry a bench and mat. This involves the children using their legs to take the strain of lifting and keeping their backs straight.

8. Large apparatus

Age range
Four to five.

Group size
Individuals.

What you need
Large apparatus, mats, benches.

What to do
On this first occasion the children will need to be shown how to get out the large apparatus. If this means that there will be little time remaining for actual activity this is not too important. If there is only a short time left (bearing in mind that all the apparatus has got to be put away again) allow the children to try quickly to find ways of travelling over, under and through the various equipment. It will also give you the chance to see whether the children have remembered the 'rules' about stopping, and it will let you and the children see what level of noise is appropriate for working.

If there is plenty of time, the children will have the opportunity to explore the apparatus in a more constructive way. This can be achieved by allowing the children full rein to discover various ways of travelling over, under and through the apparatus. This includes *all* the apparatus, not just the ropes! It may be necessary to remind the children that the mats and floor area are also part of the apparatus.

It would be very difficult to try to give specific layouts for equipment here as this will vary enormously from school

There should be at least two children per mat and two per bench.

As the children have only worked on mats so far, they will be quite excited by the new additions to the work space. Once the warm-up is completed they should sit down and be reminded of the action words they have been working with previously. The first activity the children should do is to find ways of getting over a bench or mat. Allow them the freedom to move around the whole room and every time they come to a bench or mat they must find a new way of getting over it (for example, a bunny hop).

Next, involve the children in trying to find ways of travelling along a bench or mat. They will no doubt use the ideas they got at floor level, but if they are getting stuck here are some suggestions.
• Mat – forward roll, 'sausage' roll, any of the jumps (trying to make different body shapes in the air), crab walking, bottom walking, catsprings, sliding and so on.

• Bench – rolling, either 'sausage' or forward, any of the jumps (thinking of body shape), bunny hops, bottom spins along the bench, sliding and so on.

Pick out good examples and unusual ideas to show the rest of the class. Once the children have explored the apparatus fully remind them of the action phrase – 'travel, jump, roll' – and set the task of making up a sequence using the apparatus. An example of such a sequence might be: 'The children slide along the bench, using their hands to pull themselves along, until they reach its end (make sure a mat is strategically placed there). They should then do a catspring on the bench to attain a standing position and do a two feet to two feet jump, making a star shape in the air. Upon landing (remembering to absorb the impact through their legs and feet), the children should do a forward roll to finish in a standing position.'

If time permits, let the children show their ideas to the rest of the class. If time runs short they can perfect and show their sequences in another lesson.

to school. However, as a basic guide, the following ideas can be used on the types of equipment listed below:

• flat top boxes – rolling along, jumping off;
• climbing frames – rolling around the bars, travelling up, over and through (involving body shape), swinging across where appropriate (*not* jumping from);
• benches – (these may be hooked on to apparatus to provide height) sliding, rolling and jumping on to and off are all possibilities;
• mats and floor – remind the children that these form part of the apparatus and should be used accordingly.

Quite early on you should test whether the children have remembered what to do on the command 'stop'. Noise levels will rise in this lesson so you should explain the necessity for low noise levels.

9. Devising a sequence on apparatus

Age range
Four to five.

Group size
Groups of five or six.

What you need
Large apparatus, benches, mats.

What to do
In the preceding activity the children were given the opportunity to explore and experiment on the equipment. For this activity the class should be divided into groups of five or six and each group assigned to a particular piece of apparatus. (This should consist of at least one flat surface, a piece of climbing equipment and mats – a wall bar with a bench inclined up it and a couple of mats could provide one piece.)

Remind the children of the action words 'travel, jump, roll' and set them the task of devising a sequence on their particular piece of apparatus. Stop them regularly so that you can demonstrate good movements and keep control of the class.

If there is time, ask the children to perform their completed sequences. This can be done by having one child from each piece of apparatus working while the others from that particular group watch. Try to say something positive about everyone's performance.

Further activity
You may decide to rotate the groups around the pieces of apparatus so that they can work on another sequence on the new piece.

10. Partner work

Age range
Four to five.

Group size
Pairs.

What you need
Mats.

What to do
Once the children have explored the theme of locomotion individually, introduce the idea of working with a partner. There are various ways that partner work can be carried out, but the most appropriate one to start with is copying. This involves the children working side by side and treating their partners as shadows. The child will use the same side of her body as her partner, so that if she starts to hop on her right leg her partner will also hop on her right leg.

Partner work involves a fresh dimension, so that although the children will not actually be covering new ground, they will still be progressing in gymnastic terms.

When children start working with partners it should be emphasised that movements must be kept very simple. Demonstrate, with the help of a child, that it is difficult, for example, to walk together in step at exactly the same pace. The children should be reminded that they must talk to one another as they work, but that the noise level should not rise to an unacceptable level.

Ask the children to sit in pairs. If there is an odd number of children, this sort of partner work can be done in threes. Expect quite a lot of noise because the children will need to discuss things and talk one another through their work.

Choose three action words based on the theme of locomotion and on the work already covered individually (for example, 'travel, jump, roll'). You can then allow each partnership to work by themselves on a sequence. Encourage them to work fairly slowly, at least at the beginning, and remind them that they should try to link their actions together. Also reiterate that they should work at different levels.

You may want to begin this work by letting the children work on a directed sequence to help them get started. Such a sequence may go as follows: 'travel using a sliding action on the floor followed by a catspring to a standing position; then jump from two feet to two feet making a straight body shape in the air. (On landing, remind the children to absorb the impact by bending their knees.) The sequence can finish with a forward roll'.

If you decide to give the children a free rein from the start they will probably work in a 'follow-the-leader' way. You should encourage them to progress, once the ideas have been worked out, so that they are working side by side and doing the actions at the same time.

Some examples of possible movements are:
• travel – sliding, running, walking, hopping, skipping;
• jump – five basic jumps (thinking about body shape), catspring, bunny hop;
• roll – 'sausage', forward and so on.

The children must talk and count as they work to maintain good timing. The ideal would be for them to finish up by doing their sequence at exactly the same time.

Towards the end of the lesson pick out examples of good timing to show the other children.

Further activity
If the children have followed a directed sequence, they might make up their own.

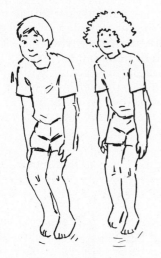

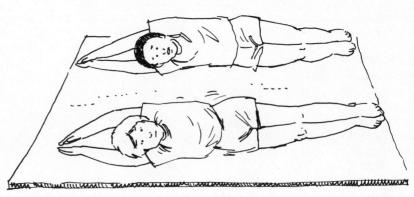

11. Partner work on low apparatus

Age range
Four to five.

Group size
Pairs.

What you need
Low apparatus such as benches and mats.

What to do
Introduce low apparatus, such as benches and mats, into the children's partner work. They should work on the same action phrase as in the previous activity – for example 'travel, jump, roll' to produce a sequence. Remind them that the benches can be used in a variety of ways – for travelling along, over and off – and that the floor area and mats should also be used.

When working on the apparatus the children should be allowed plenty of time to try out their ideas. You should pick out good examples of an action or linking movement, or good timing to demonstrate to the rest of the class. If the children progress well with their sequences, leave time at the end of the lesson to let pairs show their work. If there isn't time, or the children progress more slowly, the exercise should be carried on in the next lesson. Give the children time to revise and rehearse their sequences before they perform them.

12. Partner work on large apparatus

Age range
Four to five.

Group size
Pairs.

What you need
Large apparatus, benches, mats.

What to do
In this activity the children will once again use the action phrase 'travel, jump, roll' and work with a partner using copying, but this time they will use the large apparatus. You must decide whether to put the children on a particular piece of apparatus (try to have no more than three pairs working on each piece at a time), or whether to allow them a free choice. However, whichever method you choose, the children must make up a sequence using the action phrase and the copying form of partner work. As before, they should try to link their actions together and aim at good timing with their partners.

If the children are to show their resulting work, at least two lessons will be needed. Depending on the time available the children could rotate around the various pieces of apparatus.

Balance: 1

1. Shoulder stands and handstands

Age range
Five to six.

Group size
Individuals.

What you need
Mats.

What to do
Ask the children to travel round the room until you tell them to stop. They must then show a balance and hold it for a count of three. Let the children continue moving around the area, stopping and balancing on a different part of the body at each command of 'stop'. Pick out those children who have stopped on large bases such as their backs, hips, shoulders or stomachs, and ask them to show the rest of the class their large-base balances.

At this stage take the opportunity to teach the children a shoulder stand. To do this the child should lie flat on a mat, pushing his feet upwards and supporting his hips with his hands. His elbows should make a triangular shape.

Ask the children to move around the area again, but tell them to make their balances on small bases such as their hands, feet, heads, forearms, shins and knees, or any combination of these. Having completed this, you can show the children how to do a handstand. (**NB:** mats are essential.) There are two ways of teaching a handstand.
• Place the mat against a wall and tell the child to stand with her back to the wall. She should then put her hands down, so that they are about shoulder-width apart and walk her feet up the wall, moving her hands back towards the wall as her feet move up.
• Ask the child to spread her fingers wide and put them on the mat so that they are about shoulder-width apart. Tell the child to bounce both feet upwards, keeping her head up.

The child should repeat this, but bouncing her feet higher each time until eventually her feet are over her head. Tell the children to keep the same hand and head position as before but this time, try kicking up using one leg. This can be done against a wall or, if the child is older, by a classmate. The supporter should stand with one foot forward so that the handstander's hands are on either side of his forward foot. The supporter should hold the hips of the handstander, putting her head to one side so that when she kicks, her feet go on to the shoulder of the supporter. Children of similar build should be selected for each pairing.

Further activity
The concept of symmetry and asymmetry may be introduced. When the children are showing a balance, they should be asked whether they think it is symmetrical or asymmetrical; in other words, whether their bodies are doing the same thing on both sides. They should try to imagine folding themselves in half. Do the two sides match? If the two sides are different, the balance is asymmetrical.

Ask the children to travel around the area and this time when you ask them to stop, tell them whether they should make a symmetrical or asymmetrical balance.

2. Headstands

Age range
Five to six.

Group size
Individuals.

What you need
Mats.

What to do
Mats are essential when teaching a headstand. Tell the child to place his hands on the mat so that they are shoulder-width apart. He should spread out his fingers. Using that part of the forehead where the hair starts to grow, he should make a triangle shape on the mat with his hands and head. Tell him to keep his legs straight and then walk his feet towards his head until his hips are over his head. He should then lift his feet gently so that his heels touch his bottom. As the child grows more proficient, his legs can be straightened during the lifting phase.

Introduce the action phrase 'travel, balance, travel, balance' and tell the children that they will use this phrase to make up a movement sequence. You can either leave the size of the base for the children to decide, or you can add a restriction; for example, use a small base for the first balance and a large for the second. You could also stipulate that one of the balances must be inverted (upside down) for example, a shoulder stand, handstand or headstand.

Tell the children to pay particular attention to body shape when making a balance. The parts of their bodies which are not actually supporting their balances should look good – extended

feet, straight arms and so on. These parts of the body form the counter-balance for the balance itself.

The children might want to use twists in their sequences; for example, in a handstand, so that their legs land in a different place from where they took off. Twists can also be used to form a part of the balance, providing an interesting shape. For example, in a shoulder stand the hips and legs could be twisted and perhaps the knees bent.

Further activity
This lesson might be extended to run over a further week so that the children rehearse and then show their work.

3. Working on low apparatus

Age range
Five to six.

Group size
Individuals.

What you need
Benches, mats.

What to do
In this session the children will work on low apparatus. Ask

them to use the action phrase 'travel, balance, travel, balance' to make a sequence. Encourage them to balance on the benches, attempting inverted balances such as shoulder stands too. If you drape a mat over a bench, this may also encourage them to try headstands.

Try to persuade the children to link their actions together by reminding them that travel includes movements such as jumps, rolls, slides and so on. Allow them plenty of time to experiment with different actions and ways of linking them. Remind them to change direction (which can be achieved by twisting) and vary the speed and their body shapes as they work.

If there is time, the children should show their sequences to the rest of the class towards the end of the lesson. Otherwise, they should be allowed another lesson to work on the action phrase, remembering that they will need time to revise and rehearse their sequences before they perform them. The children should always remember to have a clear beginning and ending to their sequences.

4. Working on large apparatus

Age range
Five to six.

Group size
Individuals.

What you need
Large apparatus, benches, mats.

What to do
Using all the apparatus, the children should try to find places where they can balance; for example, box tops and wall bars. Watch carefully and pick out any good or particularly unusual ideas which show a variety of balances – large and small bases, symmetrical or asymmetrical balances, balances with twists and so on.

When the children have started to run out of ideas, reintroduce the action phrase that they used in the previous activity – 'travel, balance, travel, balance'. It may not be possible to get this far the first time you use large apparatus, especially if lots of demonstrations by the children are used; if this is the case, carry on in another session.

Emphasise to the children that body shape, speed and direction will provide interest and variety to their sequences. They should also be reminded that their work should have a clear beginning and ending.

5. Partner work

Age range
Five to six.

Group size
Pairs.

What you need
Mats.

What to do
The work previously completed on the action phrase 'travel, balance, travel, balance' can now be given an added perspective by the introduction of partner work. The children can either work by copying or you can introduce a new form of partner work – mirroring.

Tell the children to imagine a two-way mirror between themselves and their partners as they work. It will take some time for the reverse mirror image to become second nature – that is if the left hand is moved on one side of the mirror, the right hand is moved on the other side – and remember to emphasise the importance of timing and body shape. Remind the children that mirroring will be made easier by talking to each other.

Further activity
Continue with this theme, giving the children time to work on their sequences and then letting them show their work.

Once the floorwork has been satisfactorily covered, it will be time to introduce low apparatus and finally large apparatus using the action phrase and mirroring form of partner work.

Twist and turn

This theme expands those of locomotion and balance.

1. Introducing a turn

Age range
Six to seven.

Group size
Individuals.

What you need
Mats.

What to do
To start this area of work it will be necessary for the children to explore the two actions and understand the differences between them.

A turn is a movement which involves the whole body changing direction around an axis which should be thought of as a straight line through the body. For example, a jump from two feet to two feet, which starts with the child facing one direction and ends with the child facing the opposite direction after a 180° rotation, is a turn.

With a twist however, part of the body remains still while another part twists against the stationary part. Alternatively, if the twist is to be performed while the child is in motion, one part of the body must go in another direction. For example, a twist could be a jump into the air in which the legs are kept together, bent and twisted across the body by using a twist at the waist.

Having briefly explained the difference between a twist and a turn tell the children that for this lesson they will be looking at turns. Tell them that there are three different axes which may pass through their bodies in the following positions:

• from head to toe in a vertical position. For example if the children perform a jump with a 180° turn using a two feet to two feet jump. This axis may also be used in a horizontal position, with the children lying on the floor and doing a 'sausage' roll.

• horizontally through the hips (for example if the children do a forward roll), shoulders (if the children do a handstand into a forward roll), waist (if the children do a roll in a tucked position on their backs).

• through the stomach/waist/chest and out through the back – for example if the children do a cartwheel.

Only one axis at a time should be introduced and the children should do an example of each. They should try to find new and different ones and pick out any good moves and let the rest of the class try them out. The children can then move on to the next axis.

2. Twist

Age range
Six to seven.

Group size
Individuals.

What you need
Mats.

What to do
In this activity the children will explore twists. These can be done as part of a balance, or as part of movement. Ask the children to start with a large-base balance and then to twist one part of their bodies against another. They could try a shoulder stand where they bend their knees, keeping their legs together so that their knees are pointing to one side, thus producing a twist at the waist.

Once the children know what is expected of them they can go on to explore other balances which might include a twist.

Next, the children can add a twist to a movement. The simplest movement to use is a jump and the children can add a twist in mid-flight; for example, a two feet to two feet jump with the bottom half of the bodies going one way and the top half the other.

Throughout their work on the twist, the underlying sub-theme should be body shape and the children should be encouraged to develop this aspect. Direction is also important because if the twist is followed through, it generally results in a change of direction. For example, if the children do a shoulder stand with a twisted body shape and then follow the direction of the twist, they will finish up doing a backward roll over one shoulder.

Further activity
Introduce the idea of a change of speed. For example, a shoulder-stand balance could be performed as a slow movement while the follow through of the twist could be performed quickly. Another example which the children could try would be to jump, using a two feet take off, and do a twist at the waist so that their knees point to the side in mid-air. They should then land so that they are facing the same way as they were originally going. Once they have mastered this technique, they could try to do the twist as quickly as possible. If they feel like a real challenge, they could try doing two twists, so that their knees point to one side and then to the other.

3. Working on low apparatus

Age range
Six to seven.

Group size
Individuals.

What you need
Benches, mats.

What to do
Using both the benches and the mats, ask the children to try different ways of using them for doing twisting and turning actions.
• Using the bench, the children could do a shoulder stand on it, then twist and land on their knees or feet.
• Using the mat, the children could jump off a bench, adding a turn 'in the air' to land facing in a different direction. Or they could do a jump showing a twisted body shape while in flight.
• The children could roll along the bench on their stomachs, performing a 'sausage' roll and keeping as straight as possible, thus using the vertical axis from head to toe.
• The children could use the mat to explore further any action they previously performed during the floorwork.

When they have experimented on the apparatus, the children should be stopped and given the action phrase 'balance, twist, travel, jump, turn'. They can then spread out around the apparatus so that they each have a mat and bench upon which to work.

Try to have as few children as possible sharing the same mat and bench and remind them that the floor is also part of their apparatus. You should then give them plenty of time to work on their sequences.

Further activity
The activities set out above will probably take up all the available time, so the children will need part of the next session to rehearse and then perform their finished work.

Watch the sequences they have devised, reminding them beforehand that the performances should have a clear beginning and ending.

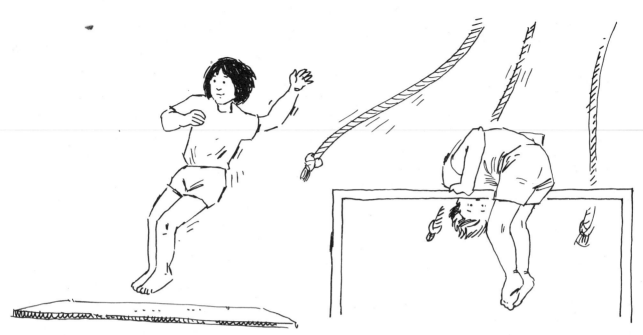

4. Working on large apparatus

Age range
Six to seven.

Group size
Individuals.

What you need
Large apparatus.

What to do
The aim of this session is to introduce the idea of twisting and turning on to apparatus. Once the children have tried out various attempts on the apparatus illustrating separate action words, they can then begin to work on the action phrase, 'balance, twist, travel, jump, turn'.

The following are suggestions for the children when trying out ideas for the action words 'twist' and 'turn'.
• The children can jump from the box tops showing either a twist or a turn during flight.

Impress on them the need to absorb the impact of the landing by bending their knees.
• They can do a head or shoulder stand with a twisted shape on top of the box.
• They can swing on the rope and then jump from the rope and turn to land facing in another direction.
• They can show a twisted shape in a balance while hanging from the ladders
• They can roll around the horizontal bars.

As they work, remind the children of the three axes they can use. You should also stop the class occasionally so that individuals can show examples of the different actions they are doing on various pieces of apparatus.

When the children begin to develop their ideas further, they should be split into groups and given a piece of apparatus so that they can work on the action phrase.

Move the groups around each piece of apparatus allowing them time to work out a sequence.

The children will need at least two weeks to work on all the pieces of apparatus and perfect their movements.

5. Partner work

Age range
Six to seven.

Group size
Pairs.

What you need
Mats.

What to do
The aim of this lesson is to introduce the theme of twist and turn into partner work, using either copying or mirroring. Ask the children to

1. Jumping into and out of balance

Age range
Seven to eight.

Group size
Individuals.

What you need
Mats.

What to do
Ask the children to twist from one action into another. For example, they can do a shoulder stand, twist over one shoulder into a knee balance (this may need a demonstration). The children could also do a shoulder stand and then push and twist upwards and sideways so that they end up in bow shape on their stomachs (a fishflop).

Tell the children to jump into a balance. For example they can do a forward roll into a balance on their bottoms, spreading out their arms and legs into a wide body shape.

2. Swinging into and out of balance

Age range
Seven to eight.

Group size
Individuals.

What you need
Mats.

What to do
The children can practise tipping from a balance. For example, they can do a one-

---

work on a sequence using the action phrase, 'twist, travel, turn'.

Make sure that the class have covered this work individually and that the children are accustomed to partner work. Remind the class that copying involves working side by side, using the same side of their bodies, while mirroring consists of working side by side, head to head or back to back, using the opposite sides of their bodies. If the children make up simple sequences they will find that they look more effective.

Ask the children to start off by working on the mats (in subsequent lessons they can move on to use small apparatus and then large apparatus). As the lesson progresses, pick out good examples of the two action words and also examples of good timing and body shapes. You should also emphasise the need for the children to change direction and perhaps

speed, so that the finished sequence is kept fairly interesting.

As the children have already explored the theme individually, there should be no need for much teacher input. However, they should be allowed plenty of time to work on their sequences and be reminded that they need a clear beginning and ending to their sequence. (If there is insufficient time in one lesson for the children to show their work they can carry on in the next lesson.)

Balance: 2

This theme has already been explored in this chapter. However, the aim here is to introduce the idea of moving into and out of a balance. For this theme, it would be advisable to work on one or two aspects each week and then set aside a week for the children to put together and show their sequences.

footed balance as described above, then they can tip over by bending their knees, putting their hands down and putting their chins on their chests and moving into a forward roll. The children might also try doing this without using their hands, but they must make sure that they look at their knee and get their chins on their chests so that their neck touches the floor first when rolling.

The children can then practise swinging into a balance. For example, they can use their hands, legs or feet to initiate a swing which results either in a jump with the landing becoming a balance, or in some movement such as a cartwheel or a handstand.

3. Making up a sequence

Age range
Seven to eight.

Group size
Individuals.

What you need
Mats.

What to do
Remembering the groundwork they have done in the previous two weeks, the children should now pick out their favourite twist, roll, tip and swing actions. They can then put all four movements together to form a sequence. Emphasise that these four actions are to be used to connect travel with balance. Before the children work on their own sequences it might be useful if they go through a directed sequence. This will ensure that they have assimilated the concept of one action leading to another.

Ask the children to start off in a standing position with their arms raised above their heads. They can then do a cartwheel or handstand leading into a forward roll. From the forward roll the children should move on to their feet, but without standing up. They should tip back and do a shoulder stand with a twist which leads to a balance on their knees.

Having worked on this sequence the children can work out their own sequences. Remind them that their sequences must have a beginning and an ending, in the form of a moment of stillness. If there is time at the end of the lesson the children can show their work. If there is not enough time, allow another week for them to rehearse, complete and show their work.

4. Using low apparatus

Age range
Seven to eight.

Group size
Individuals.

What you need
Mats, benches.

What to do
Let the children use all the apparatus to find ways of performing the required actions of the phase 'twist, roll, swing and tip (into or out of a balance or travel)'. For example, they might use a swing to initiate a jump from a bench, or the swing might initiate a twist in mid-flight with the landing taking the form of a one-footed balance. They might also decide to use a balance such as a shoulder stand and a twist which will involve tipping on to their feet and then tipping into a backward roll.

Once the children have tried out various actions, separate them into groups, so that each group can work with a set piece of apparatus. They should be allowed plenty of time to work on their sequences and then show their work.

5. Using large apparatus

Age range
Seven to eight.

Group size
Individuals.

What you need
Large apparatus.

What to do
Let the children explore all the apparatus to find ways they can twist, roll, swing, roll into and out of balances, and travel. When they have had enough time to do this, divide the class into small groups and assign each group to a particular piece of apparatus to work on their sequences. For example the children can travel on rope swings on to other apparatus, and they can also use box tops or benches to show examples of balance which could then tip them into a forward roll.

It might be advisable to teach the class one particular action, for example a tip into a roll on a box top or bench. To do this, you should first revise how to do a safe forward roll and let the children practise this on the mats. They can then transfer the action on to the apparatus. They should grip the sides of the box top or bench and this should keep them fairly straight.

Once the children have had some time to try out their ideas they should work on a sequence of 'travel, balance, twist, roll, tip, swing'. They will need to be allowed plenty of time to work out the sequences and then show their work.

6. Partner work

Age range
Seven to eight.

Group size
Pairs.

What you need
Mats.

What to do
Tell the children that they will work with partners to make up a sequence from the action phrase 'travel, balance with twist, roll, tip and swing'. To help them do this, instigate 'follow-the-leader' activities with one child in each pair doing the action while the other copies it. The children will need to be reminded to keep their ideas fairly simple. Guide them through a demonstration of this method to give them an idea of what is expected of them; for example:
• The first child slides and then does a catspring to a standing position.
• The second child then follows, repeating her actions.
• The first child tips into a forward roll, ending in a standing position.
• The second child follows, repeating her actions.
• The first child swings her arms to lead into a straight jump.
• The second child follows, repeating her actions.
• The first child tips backwards into a shoulder stand, balances showing a twist at the hips and holds this position.
• The second child follows, repeating her actions.
Having worked through an example, let the children make up their own sequences. Stop them occasionally to

demonstrate good practice and remind them that changes of direction and speed will make their sequences more interesting.

The children should be allowed plenty of time in order to work on their sequences and to show their finished work.

Further activity

If required, go on in future weeks with these ideas using low and then large apparatus.

Contract and stretch

The primary component of this theme will be body shape, but symmetry/asymmetry and dimensions will also be covered.

1. Contract and stretch

Age range

Eight to nine.

Group size

Individuals.

What you need

Mats.

What to do

Examine the principle of contraction with children. To help them understand what you mean by contraction ask them to sit down in a curled position and try to get as much of their body as possible as close to their navel as they can. Some will achieve this position but others may not be able to at first.

Next, ask the children to show a contraction around the

sides of their waists. The correct way for them to do this is to stand on one leg with the other leg raised so that it is as near to the waist as possible. The rest of the body should also be wrapped around the waist.

For the third contraction, tell the children to contract around the middle of their backs. The correct shape will be obtained by the children lying on their stomachs and putting their heads back and holding their feet up to produce a bowl shape.

So far the session will have been fairly static and so ask the children to move around the room in different directions. At intervals tell them to stop. The children should then stop and contract a part of their bodies. Pick out the best ones for demonstration.

Move on to examine stretching by giving the children several examples to do. Ask them to stand on two feet and stretch up as high as possible, keeping their arms

and legs together. Tell them to repeat this, but with only one foot on the floor. Can the children devise their own stretches with one foot on the floor? Bring in the concept of symmetry and asymmetry by asking the children to stand on one leg and stretch their arms out to their sides and one leg backwards.

Further activity

Introduce the idea of tension in both contraction and stretching. The children should try to be as strong as they can while in a stretched position. Then they can keep the same shape, but totally relax. One half of the class should watch as the other half do this and then they can swap around. What can they say about tension? Is it needed to stretch? The children can repeat this with contraction.

absorb the impact of the jump). Mats can be used for refinements of movements already initiated in the floorwork.

Remind the children about symmetry and asymmetry. They should be separated into groups and each group can be given a separate piece of apparatus on which to work individually on their sequence, using the action phrase 'contract, stretch, contract, stretch'. They can then rehearse their sequences and show them at the end of the session.

2. Action phrase

Age range
Eight to nine.

Group size
Individuals.

What you need
Mats.

What to do
Test the children's understanding of the concepts contract and stretch by asking them to make up a sequence involving both action words. The action phrase is 'contract, stretch, contract, stretch'. The children should demonstrate, through their actions, that in order to stretch some degree of contraction must have occurred beforehand.

Suggest different parts of the body which might form a base on which they can contract such as hips, knees, hands and so on. The children should be reminded about working at different levels and

speeds and you should also encourage them to add twists to their contracted movements. The children should also be given time to rehearse and then show their sequences.

3. Working with low apparatus

Age range
Eight to nine.

Group size
Individuals.

What you need
Benches, mats.

What to do
Ask the children to use all the apparatus to explore ways of performing contracting and stretching movements. They can use benches to jump from in order to perform contracted shapes during flight. Alternatively, they could use stretched body shapes during the flight. (Remind them about using the correct landing technique – their legs bent to

4. Working on large apparatus

Age range
Eight to nine.

Group size
Individuals.

What you need
Large apparatus, benches, mats.

What to do
The aim of the lesson is to use the action phrase 'contract, stretch, contract, stretch' on large apparatus. First, ask the children to explore all of the apparatus, using the actions of contract and stretch. When they have had time to do this they should be divided into groups and assigned to a piece of apparatus to work individually on their own sequences.

If the children get stuck then the following suggestions for actions on various pieces of apparatus might be useful.
• The children can use wall bars to show a stretched position moving into a contracted one. They should

hang by their hands, stretching and then drawing their knees up to show a contraction around their navels.

• The children can use box tops and benches to show flight with either a stretch or a contraction. Box tops can also be used to roll on (a contraction); leading to a stretch such as straddling the box with their legs wide and arms stretched, making a symmetrical star-shape, or a twist to make a three-dimensional shape.

• The very act of climbing a rope involves the child in contraction and stretching.

• The children can use ladders to show a stretch. By using different body shapes they can use these actions to show dimensions, symmetry and asymmetry.

Further activity
At least two weeks should be spent on this theme, and another week should be devoted to the children showing their work.

5. Partner work

Age range
Eight to nine.

Group size
Pairs.

What you need
Mats.

What to do
The aim of this session is for the children to use the action phrase 'contract, stretch, contract, stretch' to make a sequence with a partner. They should be encouraged to talk to one another as they work and the best method of

working they can adopt is copying.

Ask the children to devise methods of stretching and contracting, wherever possible using symmetry and asymmetry. Pick out good examples to show the rest of the class. The children should then try to link the stretches and contractions together by using travel, sliding, rolling, jumping and so on.

Allow the children plenty of time to work on their sequences and then let them show their completed work.

Flight

1. Developing jumping

Age range
Nine to ten.

Group size
Individuals.

What you need
Mats.

What to do
The aim of this session is to take the action of jumping further so that it leads to emphasised flight. However,

start off by reminding the children of the five basic jumps (see page 82).

Let the children demonstrate each type of jump and then show them how they should recover from each one. There are two ways to recover from a jump:
• on balance
• off balance.

To make a balanced landing the child should start with a balance, then jump and land on both feet so that his knees are slightly bent to absorb the impact. Introduce the concept of the centre of gravity being low and therefore the child should imagine sinking into the floor on landing. He should also keep his hips and bottom as low as he can as he lands. Stress the idea that the child must be in control of his body so that he can land in a balanced way.

Next, the children should move on to find out about landing off balance. Even so, tell the children that there must still be an element of control in their landings. Such landings will involve the use of a running jump, albeit at a fairly slow pace. On landing the children should continue

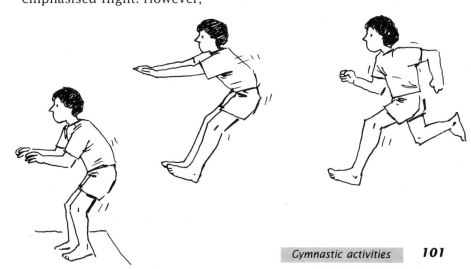

running and gradually decelerate to stop.

The children should also try rolling and landing, making sure that there are enough thick mats to cushion such landings. Most children will start with a sideways roll. Later on you can introduce the dive roll landing. The thickness of the mats available will determine how high the children should be allowed to dive. A crash mat would be needed for a high dive while standard mats would only allow a pounce into the roll.

Remind the children how to do a proper forward roll from a standing position (see page 82). Then the children can start the dive part of the roll by doing a little jump into the roll. They should be reminded that their hands and arms will absorb the impact of the landing and that they must keep their chins tucked into their chests so that the backs of their necks, or even their shoulders touch the mat. They must not land on the top of their heads. The children

should stand with their feet up to the edge of the mat and with their arms outstretched. Tell them to pounce on to their hands and roll, keeping their heads well tucked in. Ask them to keep practising this technique but they should continue to add height to the initial pounce. You can help them to do this by using a cane or an arm as a barrier for them to drive over. Once the children are proficient at this, they can add a small run up, gradually increasing the speed.

Further activity

If you feel that the children are sufficiently confident, you can use the dive roll as an introduction to vaulting. You will need to use a spring, in which the child lands on the box on her hands and the back of her neck and then uses her legs to 'flick' herself over the box in a forward roll. It will be necessary to support the child's first attempts. To do this stand to one side of the box and use one hand to support the shoulder and the other hand to clutch a handful of clothing at the child's waist or hip level. Guide the vaulter to the floor and hold on to the child until balance is regained,

stopping any forward rotation.

When this technique has been mastered the children can try a headspring where they place their hands and the tops of their heads on to the box as in a headstand. They can also try a short-arm vault and a long-arm vault which are a kind of handstand performed over the box, using either bent arms or straight arms.

2. High jumps

Age range
Nine to ten.

Group size
Individuals.

What you need
Mats.

What to do
Introduce the children to the idea of jumping, as high as they can, and encourage them to use various parts of their bodies to initiate or gain height. Start off by asking them to use their hands and arms as the initiators by swinging them upwards as they jump. Tell them to do a two feet to two feet jump and try to get as high as possible.

Next, the children should use their legs to gain height. Tell them to use a two feet to one foot jump, bending the knees of the take-off leg and swinging their other leg upwards at the same time, twisting their bodies to land after making a 180° turn.

Stress the importance of landing safely; the children's legs must be bent to absorb the impact of their landing.

As the children develop ideas, begin to stress the importance of body shape. Ask them to find as many different

positions as they can during flight – tucked, twisted, stretched, symmetrical and asymmetrical and so on.

Further activity
Ask the children to find other parts of their bodies from which to take off. Remind them to use their arms and legs to gain height.

3. Introducing an action phrase

Age range
Nine to ten.

Group size
Individuals.

What you need
Mats.

What to do
Encourage the children to add structure to their work by introducing the action phrase, 'travel, jump, travel, jump', and asking them to make up a sequence. Their first attempts should be directed by you so that you give them an idea of what you expect. Therefore, ask the children to run into a dive roll. (This may be modified for those children who have not yet mastered the dive roll, or for those schools without crash mats, by having them slide to the mat, do a catspring to a standing position and then do a pouncing movement into the roll.)

They should finish the roll in a standing position and then twist their bodies round slowly, making a 180° twist, so that their feet are the last part of their bodies to turn. Tell them to sink to the floor and do a shoulder stand. They should get out of the shoulder stand by twisting over one shoulder into a backward roll, and then into a standing position.

Finally, ask the children to do a symmetrical star jump, using their arms to gain height. They should land and hold this position to show the end of their sequence.

Give the children time to rehearse their work and then show their sequences. They can then be encouraged to make up their own sequences using the action phrase. Allow them plenty of time to work on their sequences and then ask them to show their finished work.

4. Working on low apparatus

Age range
Nine to ten.

Group size
Individuals.

What you need
Benches, mats.

What to do
This will be the first time the children work on apparatus using this theme, so to begin with, let them try out all the equipment using the action words, 'jump' and 'travel'. Benches will obviously add height to the children's jumps, but make sure that they land safely on a mat, bending their knees to absorb the impact. The children can also jump and do dive rolls over the benches, providing the mats are sufficiently thick.

Once the children have had enough time to explore, encourage them to work on the sequences they explored at floor level. They can adapt these to make use of all the apparatus. For example, if they had a jump in their sequence in the floorwork, the children could do the jump off the bench. Keep reminding the children of the sub-themes of level, direction, body shape and speed as they work.

The children should be allowed time to rehearse and show their finished sequences.

5. Working on large apparatus

Age range
Nine to ten.

Group size
Individuals.

What you need
Large apparatus, benches, mats.

What to do
The aim of this activity is to work on the theme of flight on large apparatus. This latter opens up all sorts of possibilities, so it is worth spending a lesson with the children exploring these.
• The children can use ropes to 'fly' on to and off other pieces of apparatus, and also on to and off the actual rope itself.
• They can use flight on to and off ladders using swinging movements.
• They can use box tops to 'fly' on to, off and over.
• They can use flight off the wall bars by swinging on them.
• They can use flight on to the pole leading to such movements as falling around the pole.
• They can use flight on to, off and over benches.
• Mats are not only useful for landing on, but can also be used by the children to 'fly' over.

At all times stress to the children the importance of using the correct landing technique. This can be emphasised by stopping the children every so often to show their good ideas, good landing positions and so on. This will also help with the safety aspect of the activity emphasising to the children that they must stop when they are told.

Further activity
The action phrase 'travel, jump, travel, jump' can be introduced. The children should be given time to work on their sequence, refining and rehearsing it and finally showing their finished work. Remember that all work should have a definite beginning and ending.

Different forms of partner work

By now the children will be quite used to working with a partner. However, so far the children have used partners to complement one another. At this stage the aim is for the children to use partners to do work which would not be possible on their own, in other words they will be using their partners as obstacles. The actions used will be those the children explored in earlier years.

1. Travel and balance

Age range
Ten to eleven.

Group size
Pairs.

What you need
Mats.

What to do
Balance and travel lend themselves well to partner work. Ask the children to get into pairs. They should then start by one child making a shape, for example a star shape. Their partners must find some way of going under this shape, for example sliding, rolling and so on. The

children can then swap over so that the shape-maker becomes the active partner. Can they find a different way of going under their partners? Can the children now think of some shapes and methods of travelling over, under, round or through the barrier their partners have created?

Remind the children to think very carefully about the levels they are working at. The level at which the shape is made will determine the movements possible to the partner who has to negotiate it.

Once the children have had time to work on their ideas they should think of ways in which they could present a sequence, using the action phrase 'travel, balance, travel, balance'. Suggest that the children use a type of 'follow-the-leader' technique, in which one child makes a shape, her partner negotiates it and then makes the same shape for the shape-maker to negotiate; for example:
• the first child does a shoulder stand with her legs spread;
• the second child does a jump through his partner's legs, stands from the roll, turns 180° and sinks to the floor to do a shoulder stand;
• the first child meanwhile has twisted into a backwards roll over one shoulder, stood up and is ready to do a jump through the legs of her partner.

Let the children devise their own sequences using the action phrase. The work done in previous years should have built up a repertoire of movements and ideas which

will enable them to devise an interesting piece of work. Once completed the children can show their work.

2. Counter-balance and counter-tension

Age range
Ten to eleven.

Group size
Pairs.

What you need
Mats.

What to do
The aim of this activity is to introduce counter-balance and counter-tension as a form of partner work. Explain to the children that they will be exploring balances which would not be possible if they were working on their own.

Ask the children to stand facing their partners and then place their palms together and push against each other, while at the same time walking away from each other. They will either fall down or they should lock together so that they are

standing as far apart as they can get, thus achieving a counter-tension. This particular action is also possible when done back-to-back. Here the children lean against one another and gradually walk their feet outwards until they are finely balanced. Tell the children to sit back-to-back with their partners and link arms at the elbows. They should bend their knees, so that their feet are near their bottoms and then push against each other until they are in a standing position.

During initial experimentation you should emphasise that the children's actions must involve a balance which, if their partner were not there, they could not achieve by themselves.

In the examples given above, the children are either pushing or pulling against each other. In counter-balance the children are balancing on one another. For example, tell one child to lie on the floor on her back with her legs in the air, and her feet and legs together. Tell the second child to sit on the first child's feet and try to balance.

Alternatively, the second child could put her hips on the first child's feet, which should be turned outwards with the heels together. The first child should then put her arms straight up and holds hands with her partner achieving a balance in this way.

Let the children try out their own ideas for counter-balancing. They should then try to make a series of movements which are linked together, perhaps including other forms of partner work such as copying or mirroring, to achieve a sequence. They could use an action phrase such as 'travel, balance, travel, balance', repeating it several times and adding linking movements.

Further activity

Both the obstacle and the counter-tension and counter-balance forms of partner work can be expanded by using low and large apparatus. The children should find it a challenge to try to discover ways of adapting their ideas from the floorwork, and of course creating new ideas only possible on apparatus.

3. Group work

Age range
Ten to eleven.

Group size
Small groups.

What you need
Several mats per group.

What to do
The children can now try working in small groups. Allow them to form their own groups and then let them mix any type of partner work they have previously covered. Keep the action phrase very simple, for example, 'travel, jump, roll', as this will allow the children to concentrate on developing the group relationship.

To begin with, the children may benefit from being directed so that they will be able to see what is expected of them. Ask the groups to stand around the edge of the mats facing the mats. They should then all do a forward roll into the centre of the mats – making sure there are no collisions. They should then stand up from the roll and, keeping an upright stance, walk into a formation of three children at the front, all facing forwards, and the others in a

line behind them. (The children should be reminded that if they have a set number of steps to get to their positions, then those with the furthest to go should take larger steps than those only going a short distance). The children in the second row should stand in the gaps, so that the formation looks like this:

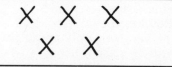

Tell the children in the front line to kneel on all fours, with their arms and knees spread out and their heads up. The children in the back line should then take a step forward and using their feet and hands, climb on to the hips and shoulders of the children in the front line. The children on top must put their feet and hands on the hips and shoulders of their supporters and not in the middle of their backs. The supporters must establish a firm and stable base so that they are supporting securely.

The balance may mark the end of the sequence, or you can ask the children being supported to jump backwards off the front line, land and stand, while the front line use a catspring to jump into a standing position. Timing is essential and it is best if just one child does any calling out of commands.

Having worked on the directed sequences, the children can make up their own sequences. They will need lots of time to perfect the timing and group shapes but once they are satisfied they should show their work to the rest of the class.

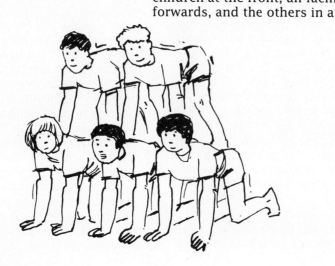

CHAPTER 5

Outdoor and adventurous activities

The National Curriculum requires that at Key Stage 2, children should be encouraged to explore the potential for physical activities within their immediate environment, undertaking simple orientation activities and applying their physical skills on such equipment as climbing frames. Children should be taught the principles of outdoor safety and profitably together with the physical and mental skills necessary to experience, safely, exciting and challenging activities.

The aim of this chapter is to provide children with a number of activities which will prepare them for, and allow them to profit from, the camping, rambling, orienteering and exploratory projects which may be designed for them.

More than any other aspect of the PE curriculum, this strand may be linked with other subject areas such as geography, science, maths and health education.

Warm-up activities

It will not be possible for children to warm-up before every activity, as some of these will take place in confined spaces or on uneven surfaces, where too much spontaneous movement might prove hazardous. However, before working on activities which take place in the playground, hall or school field, a vigorous warm-up activity should always be introduced. Choose appropriate activities from those used in other chapters, or from the list below.

• Skipping with a hoop instead of a rope.

• Running to taped music, changing the rhythm frequently.
• Running round a hoop as many times as possible before it falls.
• Balancing a bean bag on the feet and trying to flip it over the head.
• Running and changing the length of strides on command.
• Playing chain tag where the first child catches the second and holds hands, and so on until the whole class is linked.
• Bowling hoops around obstacles.
• Galloping sideways.
• Free running while bouncing a ball with one hand and catching it with the other.
• Playing chariot running where two children link arms and a third child stands

behind, grasping the linked arms and 'driving' the chariot.
• Playing circle chase where half the class stands in a circle and the other children stand behind a partner in the circle. On the command, the children standing behind run clockwise round the circle and try to end up with their hands on their partners' shoulders.
• Playing chain racing where the children link arms in fours and gallop sideways.
• Running across a classroom or playground, leaping from one hoop to another placed on the floor.
• Playing 'wood' tag where on the command 'go' the children run and touch something made of wood before the command 'stop'. Change the word to stone, grass and so on, to suit.

ACTIVITIES

1. Exploring the playground

Age range
Seven to eight.

Group size
Individuals and pairs.

What you need
Playground space.

What to do
Tell the children that you want them to look at the playground as if they have never seen it before – they are going to explore it. Tell them to work on their own and ask them to move around the playground finding places where they can stand in safety with their feet off the ground. Emphasise the importance of taking no risks. How high can they get from the ground in safety? How many different positions can they adopt on their perches? Which parts of their bodies can they balance on? What shapes can they make?

Allow the children plenty of time to discover perches, stopping them to point out those children who have found really ingenious uses of space. Then call them all together again and ask them to see how many places in the playground they can find which they can push against. How many different ways of pushing can they find? Which parts of their bodies can they push with?

Next, ask the children to find patterns in the

playground. Can they find straight lines between two objects and move along them in a variety of ways? Can they work out the shape of a square or a rectangle between walls and move in this pattern on different parts of their bodies? Can they make these movements first heavily and then lightly?

Ask the children to work in pairs. Can they find anything in the playground which they can move from one place to another? In how many ways can they carry these objects? Make sure that they put the objects back again when the session is over.

The pairs can then choose a specific area of the playground in which to work. Ask them how many movement activities they can carry out in this area – such as jumping, running, lifting, crawling, hopping – without bumping into any other children.

Further activity
The above activities can also be carried out inside the school. Take small groups of children around the building, asking them to use their eyes and move over, under, through and past any objects they encounter.

2. Using apparatus in the playground

Age range
Seven to eight.

Group size
Individuals, pairs and small groups.

What you need
Light apparatus such as hoops, ropes, skittles, quoits, balls and so on.

What to do
Ask the children to carry the apparatus into the playground and to put it on the ground. Ask the children to form groups of four or five, and make each team responsible for a different type of apparatus. Ask all the children to place their apparatus around the playground, so that, for example, all the balls are in one place, all the hoops in another and so on. Tell them that you want the apparatus distributed sensibly, so that children can use it without getting in the way of another team.

Allow the children some time to accomplish this, noting how well they work together within their teams and what degrees of collaboration there are between different groups. Finally, check that the apparatus has been distributed in a sensible manner and praise the groups who have organised their apparatus well.

Ask each group to demonstrate how well it has organised its apparatus on the ground. Can the children move easily without touching any of the apparatus in their section?

Having done this, the children should be allowed to work in their groups and use the apparatus freely and then, at a signal, move on to the next type of apparatus. When the children have experimented with all the apparatus, tell them that you are going to give each group just a few minutes to move their apparatus again. This time you want the children to design a picture from their apparatus. They can make a pattern, the shape of a bird or an animal, a geometrical shape or anything that takes their fancy. Allow them a few minutes to discuss this and then set them to work.

At the end of the session make sure that the children collect all the pieces of apparatus and return them to the store or classroom.

Further activity

The children will need two or three sessions to complete this activity. When they have grown accustomed to moving and using the apparatus, at the end of one lesson suggest that all the children collaborate using all the pieces of apparatus to make a gigantic face on the ground.

3. Moving with care

Age range
Seven to eight.

Group size
Individuals and pairs.

What you need
Light apparatus such as mats, skittles, hoops, ropes, quoits and so on.

What to do
Ask the children to distribute all the pieces of apparatus over the surface of the playground or a specific marked area of the playground. Tell them that you want to see as little space beneath and between the apparatus as possible.

After they have done this, tell the children that you want them to move about the area. Remind them that it is important to take care and move sensibly and therefore they should work without bumping into one another or touching any of the pieces of

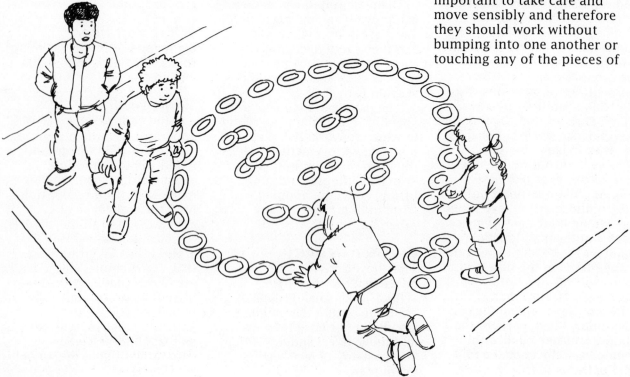

apparatus with any parts of their bodies.

The children can start off walking, but as they move tell them to change the way they move – walking backwards, walking sideways, running, running backwards, running sideways, hopping on both feet, hopping on alternate feet, skipping and so on. Encourage the children to change direction as well – straight lines, circles, squares, zigzags and so on. Towards the end of this activity allow the children to choose their own forms of movement, using as many parts of their bodies as possible to help them move.

Finish this activity by putting the children into pairs and asking them to devise ways of moving through the apparatus together. Throughout the session look for intelligent use of space, good style of movement and common sense. Praise these where they are in evidence and ask the children concerned to demonstrate them to the rest of the class.

4. Simple orienteering

Age range
Seven to eight.

Group size
Individuals or pairs.

What you need
Pieces of paper with different locations in school written on them, four quoits placed in each location.

What to do
Tell the children that you are going to give each of them a piece of paper with the name of a different part of the school written on it. Ask the children to study this and work out the quickest way of reaching the area without going through any classrooms, disturbing anyone else, or going near the road or

anywhere else which is likely to be dangerous. Tell them that when they reach their destination they will find three or four quoits there. They should bring *one* quoit back to you.

Once the children have studied their paper and worked out a route, send them off. When each child has returned with one of the quoits, redistribute the papers containing the locations and send each child off to another destination, until each has brought back another quoit. Continue this until all the rings have been collected.

Further activity
Tell the children that quoits of a certain colour are hidden all

over the playground and inside the school (in places where no children are working). Let the children work in pairs to find at least one coloured quoit. See which pair can collect the most quoits in a certain time.

5. Using a climbing frame

Age range
Seven to eight.

Group size
Individuals.

What you need
Outdoor climbing frame.

What to do
Allow the children to explore the climbing frame. Tell them that at no stage must they ever touch another child while on the frame. Ask them to devise different ways of getting on to the frame from any point and then from a fixed point. Ask them to think of different ways

of getting off the frame, first from any point and then from a fixed point.

How many different parts of their bodies can the children rest on the frame, putting all their weight on this particular part? Ask them to devise ways of hanging from different sections of the frame, letting go and landing lightly. Can they hang from their hands? Ask them to find other ways of hanging from the frame. On the frame itself, how many stretched-out positions can they adopt? How many curled-up postures can they think of?

Allow the children plenty of time to experiment and change positions on the frame, never asking a child to do more than she feels capable of.

End the session by asking the children to show you as many different ways as they can of:
• moving from the ground to the frame and from the frame to the ground;
• moving along the frame;
• moving up the frame and down the frame;
• moving under and over the frame.

NB: Only a few children should use a climbing frame at the same time. Other children should work on other pieces of apparatus or in other areas of the playground.

6. Using the playground for movement activities

Age range
Seven to eight.

Group size
Individuals and the whole class.

What you need
Playground space.

What to do
Encourage the children to use the natural attributes of the playground as the basis for movement activities. Start by asking the children to face a wall and then to imagine that they are climbing along a narrow ledge against a cliff face. They must try to dig their hands and fingers into any holes in the wall and move very slowly, extending one

foot sideways first and then bringing the second foot up to the first, before moving the first foot again. When the children come to the end of the 'ledge' they must make a long sideways leap in order to reach safety. If there are any window-sills in the wall tell the children that they must get past these as quickly as possible without being seen by anyone inside the school.

How many different ways can the children think of in which they can move while staying close to the ground? They could crawl, crouch or hop, be dragged by a partner, or use many other different forms of progress.

Ask the children to devise ways of getting quickly from one side of the playground to another using different forms of movement – hopping, skipping, walking backwards and so on. Ask them to start moving across the playground while keeping as close to the ground as they can, but to progressively straighten up, so that by the time they reach the far end they are walking as tall as they can. They should finish of with a jump.

Ask the children to move around the perimeter of the playground as quickly as they can, but making as little noise as possible. Any child who can be heard moving should be taken out of the game.

Tell the children to find a sloping part of the playground. They should imagine that it is much steeper than it really is. How are they going to move up this steep slope? What sort of movement would be best?

Finish by asking the children to work together to form shapes in the middle of the playground. Can they make a star shape, a square and a cross? What other shapes can they make as a class?

7. Constructing a shelter

Age range
Seven to eight.

Group size
Small groups.

What you need
Benches, mats of various sizes, skipping ropes, skittles.

What to do
Make a collection of apparatus in the playground and divide the children into teams of four. Tell the class that you want each group to use the pieces of apparatus to build a temporary shelter.

Ask the children to think about the things their shelters will need. They will need some sort of roof and they will have to be big enough to enable the children to get in underneath the roof.

Allow the children to discuss this in their groups and then to collect the pieces of apparatus they will need, in an orderly fashion. Supervise and encourage the children as they work and, when the shelters have been built, allow the groups to look at each others shelters and see if they can improve upon the work of the original builders.

8. Movement of apparatus

Age range
Seven to eight.

Group size
Individuals, pairs and small groups.

What you need
Benches, skittles, ropes, balls and other pieces of apparatus.

What to do
Allow the children to practise moving and setting up apparatus. Organise the children into groups and pairs and ask them to move portable apparatus from the school out into the playground and set it up so that it can be used in the playground.

Help the children to move the apparatus safely, emphasising that it should always be carried, never dragged. Ask the children if they can think of any logical places for the apparatus to be placed in the playground. For example, balls should be placed so that they can't be thrown over fences and lost and benches and jumping frames should be positioned so that when they are used no one bumps into walls.

Allow the children to use the different pieces of apparatus and then ask them to organise how it is returned into the school, making sure it is stored neatly.

9. Mapping the school

Age range
Seven to eight.

Group size
Individuals.

What you need
Paper, pencils, photocopiable page 180.

What to do
Start by asking the children to make simple maps of their classroom using photocopiable page 180.They should jot down what they can see and then make a fair copy and colour it in. They should include the position of such things as desks and chairs in the mapping.

Having done this, take the children for a walk round the school and ask them to make maps of certain areas. At this stage do not expect them to be able to make a map of the whole school, this will come later. Ask them to locate any doors and windows and to include any fixed apparatus that might be in the playground. The children should then make fair copies of all their maps.

Ask the children to work out the quickest routes within the school from one area to another. For example, the hall to the playground, the headteacher's office to the staffroom and so on. When the children have plotted their routes, ask them to follow them and decide whether they have really chosen the quickest way.

10. Fire-drill

Age range
Eight to nine.

Group size
Individuals and pairs.

What you need
Pencils, paper.

What to do
Wait until there is a school fire-practice. When one occurs, ask the children in your class to observe carefully what they do and what the children in other classes seem to do during the drill.

When the drill is over and the children have returned to the classroom discuss what they have just done and seen. What route did the class follow from the classroom to the

outside of the school? What was the reason for going this way? Is there a better way of getting out of the classroom easily? Ask the children to draw a map showing how they got from the classroom to the playground during fire-practice.

Take the children round the school and discuss the routes followed by the other classes from their classrooms to the playground. When you return to the classroom ask the children to sketch the routes the other classes follow when the fire-bell goes.

Organise the children into pairs and tell them to imagine that they cannot leave the classroom through the usual exit when there is a fire, because the fire is between them and the usual door. Ask the pairs to go round the school examining alternatives and charting another route which the class could follow safely if the usual way cannot be used.

Discuss the routes proposed by the different pairs and choose the most suitable one.

11. Expeditions

Age range
Eight to nine.

Group size
The whole class.

What you need
Pencils, paper, photocopiable page 181.

What to do
Take the children on a number of short walks to places of local interest which are within easy reach of the school for example a church, fire station, police station, supermarket

and so on. Ask the children to use photocopiable page 181 to help them sketch their route.

When the children return from each walk ask them to draw maps to show how to get from the school to the place they visited and back again, in safety, without crossing too many roads and keeping away from heavy traffic.

A little later, take the same walks again, but this time use the maps drawn by the children. How readable and accurate are they? Return to the classroom and discuss all the maps, using the board to make salient points.
Finally ask the children to make fair copies of the definitive maps of the various walks.

12. Road signs

Age range
Eight to nine.

Group size
Individuals and the whole class.

What you need
Pencils, paper, art and craft materials, photocopiable page 182.

What to do
Take the children out to look at a set of traffic lights and road signs. When you return to the classroom ask the children to complete photocopiable page 182 and discuss the sequence of traffic lights – red, red and amber, green, amber – and talk about the meaning of main traffic signs. (It may also provide an opportunity to talk about the Green Cross Code.)

Ask the children to design and make their own set of traffic lights. They can paint on the lights setting them permanently at red and amber. Also ask them to draw any three traffic signs and to write down what they mean.

Further activity
Ask the crossing patrol attendant to come in to the school and talk to the children about her work. You can integrate this with any police liaison activities.

14. Travelling through school

Age range
Eight to nine.

Group size
Individuals and small groups.

What you need
No special requirements.

What to do
Ask the children to use their knowledge of the school to devise a plan which will enable them to travel from one end of the school, for as far as possible, without touching the floor. They may use any pieces of furniture already in place and they can also travel over mats, as long as the surface of the floor is not touched.

Emphasise that safety is of the utmost importance and that they must not take any risks. Allow each child 20 seconds or so to get started before allowing the next child to begin.

When every child has had a chance to travel in this way collect the class together and discuss the methods they used. Praise those children who were particularly careful in their planning and execution of the project.

Place the children in teams of four and tell them that this time they must travel, in teams, from one end of the school to the other for as far as they can without touching the floor. Team members may help one another to stay off the ground.

When all teams have completed their trips call the class together and ask the more successful teams to talk about and demonstrate their methods.

13. The Green Cross Code

Age range
Eight to nine.

Group size
The whole class and small groups.

What you need
Chalk.

What to do
Take the children into the playground and go through the basic rules of the Green Cross Code. Draw a line with chalk to represent the kerb and tell the children to stand well back from this kerb.

Tell the children that before they attempt to cross the road they should always find a safe, quiet place, preferably a zebra crossing, a subway, or something similar. Standing back from the kerb they should look for traffic and listen for it, allowing any traffic to pass before they move. When they are sure that the way is clear they may pass across the road, walking steadily, not running.

Allow the children time to practise these manoeuvres. When you are sure they are ready, take them out to a quiet street, preferably one with a zebra crossing or a pelican crossing, and allow them to try out their crossing techniques.

NB: Either take the class out in small groups, *or* if the whole class is taken, make sure that there is at least one adult supervisor to every four or five children in the class.

Further activity

The team game can be repeated in the playground. See how long it takes each team to cross the playground with no more than two children in each team having their feet on the ground at any given time.

15. Moving a bench

Age range

Eight to nine.

Group size

Groups of six.

What you need

Light benches.

What to do

Organise the class into teams and give each team a light bench to carry out into the playground. Tell them that they have seven minutes to carry the benches as far as possible across the playground and through any other safe spaces within the school. All the children in each team must help carry the bench and every time you shout 'stop' the children must put the bench down on the ground and think of a way to move along the bench from one end to the other – sliding, dragging, hopping, running and so on. Every time that 'stop' is called, the teams must adopt a different movement. Credit will be given for the most ingenious movements along the bench, as well as for the distance the bench is carried.

Repeat this game using hoops, mats and other pieces of apparatus each time.

16. Measuring

Age range

Eight to nine.

Group size

Pairs.

What you need

Trundle wheels, measuring tapes, paper, pencils.

What to do

Let the children work in pairs and ask them to measure certain areas of the school and to record these measurements. These areas could include:
• the length and width of the classroom;
• the length and width of the hall;
• the length and width of the playground.

Ask two or three pairs to measure each area, so that the measurements may be compared and checked against each other.

Complete the session by asking the children to draw rough sketch maps showing the areas they measured.

17. Cycling

Age range

Eight to nine.

Group size

Individuals.

What you need

Bicycles, skittles, photocopiable page 183.

What to do

Try to arrange for each child to bring his bicycle to school. For children living some distance from the school this may involve asking parents to bring the bikes in at a stipulated time.

Assemble the children and their bikes in the playground

and stress the safety factors needed for safe cycling. Ask the children to check their bicycles using the check-list provided on photocopiable page 183. Try to involve the community police officer in this checking.

Let the children practise cycling slowly round the playground. They should ride in spaced single file. Set out several skittles on the ground. At the first skittle the child should make a clear arm signal, having first looked round to check that the way is clear, and turn right. At the second skittle the child should repeat the safety checks and signal and turn left. Make sure that the children keep both hands on the handlebars unless they are signalling, and both feet on the pedals.

Praise examples of good cycling and ask these children to demonstrate to the others.

This activity will probably occupy several sessions.

18. Mending a puncture

Age range
Eight to nine.

Group size
Pairs.

What you need
Bicycle with old tyre and inner tube, cycle repair kit, bucket of water.

What to do
You will either need a bicycle tyre with a puncture or you will have to puncture an old tyre for this activity. Show the children the punctured tyre and turn the bicycle upside down. Tell them that you will show them how to mend a puncture. The stages in this process are as follows:
• Unscrew the wheel hub nuts and lift the wheel free of the chain. See if there are holes or nails in the tyre and mark the spot.
• Lever the tyre away from the rim until the tyre is free.

• Undo the valve and take out the inner tube.
• Pump up the inner tube and take it through a bucket of water, a section at a time. If air bubbles indicate a hole, dry the spot and mark it with chalk.
• Let out the air, sandpaper the spot by the hole, apply glue and put on a patch. Allow it to dry.
• Push the valve through the rim and screw on the nut. Fit the tube around the rim and put the tyre over it.
• Use tyre levers to push the edge of the tyre into the rim.
• Pull the tyre into place with your hand.
• Pump up the tyre. Put the wheel back on. Hold the wheel straight between the forks. Tighten the nuts and spin the wheel. Make sure that it revolves freely.

While the other children are cycling and performing other activities, let two children at a time have a go at mending a puncture, helping them where necessary. When all the children have grasped the technique you could use spare moments in other sessions to time each pair. How long does it take each couple to mend a puncture?

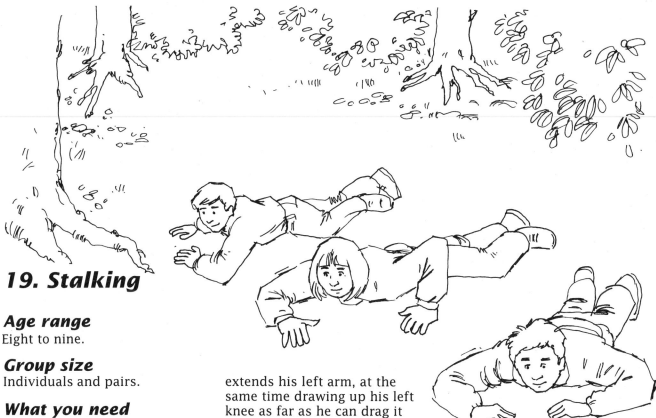

19. Stalking

Age range
Eight to nine.

Group size
Individuals and pairs.

What you need
PE shoes, dark clothing or trainers.

What to do
Take the children out to a wooded area and teach them how to stalk one another by moving quietly without being observed. Show the children how to walk quietly on the balls of the feet and let them practise walking quietly among the trees.

Show the children several basic crawls.
• The pull crawl consists of a child lying on her stomach with her arms extended on the ground in front of her head. She then digs her hands into the ground and pulls her inert body forward.
• The fast crawl consists of a child lying on his stomach on the ground with his arms by his sides. To start moving he extends his left arm, at the same time drawing up his left knee as far as he can drag it over the ground. He then draws up his right knee and places it in front of his left knee. At the same time the child swings his right arm in front of his left arm, and keeps moving continuously in this fashion, keeping as near to the ground as possible.
• The monkey run consists of a child moving on her knees and clenched fists over the ground as quickly as possible.

Give the children time to practise all three crawls until they seem to have grasped the principles of the movements. Organise the group into pairs and ask one child to crawl up behind the other child without being heard. If the first child hears the second child he should turn round and face him. Make sure that the children swap roles.

End the session with a game of hide and seek. Half the children should hide among the trees while the other half can look for their partners.

20. Tents

Age range
Nine to ten.

Group size
Pairs.

What you need
Old sheets, pieces of canvas, pegs, thin rope, mallets, string.

What to do
If there is a school field or the class has access to some open

grass, the children can be given an introduction to basic tent construction as a preparation for the camping expeditions they may be making later.

Tell them to tie a length of thin rope between two trees. They should make the rope as long as possible so that a number of pairs may work at the same time. Give each pair an old sheet or piece of canvas and tell the children that you want to see them devise and construct a basic tent in which it would be possible to shelter.

There are a number of options open to the children. Some will merely throw the sheet or canvas over the rope, with an equal amount of material falling on either side of the rope, and then peg the edges of the tent down. Other children may start by throwing the sheet over the rope, but pull it so that one side is pegged down, but the other extends only half way to the ground. This can then be kept in place with string tied to the two edges of the flaps, extending down to two pegs hammered into the ground. This version will enable the occupants to see out through the side, while still being sheltered from the sun or rain.

Give the children time to experiment with different variations, helping and encouraging them as they work.

21. Tyres playground

Age range
Nine to ten.

Group size
Small groups.

What you need
Old tyres.

What to do
Collect as many old car tyres as you can. Check them for safety, making sure that there are no protruding nails and so on. Tell the children that you want them to turn the playground into an adventure playground, using the tyres as their basic material.

Divide the children into groups of four or five and put each group in charge of a pile of tyres. Patrol the area constantly, making sure that the children are working safely and that they are lifting the tyres in groups, not on their own. Encourage the class to devise their own elements for the adventure playground. Stop the children every now and then and ask them to demonstrate any ingenious ideas.

Among the uses the children may find for the tyres might be:
• obstacle races, with children jumping from tyre to tyre, or running, placing their feet inside each tyre;
• tunnels, placed end to end, for children to crawl through;
• competitions to see how high a structure may be built from tyres;
• giant hoopla, using the tyres as receptacles for cushions thrown from a distance.

Further activity
Using the tyres as the basis of the adventure playground the children could be asked to look for other objects which could be included such as ropes, cardboard boxes and so on.

22. Fishing

Age range
Nine to ten.

Group size
Individuals and pairs.

What you need
Canes, lengths of nylon line, curtain rings, fish hooks, tape.

What to do
Introduce the children to fishing by helping them to make fishing rods and taking them in groups on a fishing expedition.

Show the children a simple fishing rod and then let them work in pairs to make two basic rods between them. Give each pair several lengths of cane, some nylon line, curtain rings, tape and fish hooks. Ask each pair of children to design their rods and then build them.

Children may have a variety of different ideas, but most of them will probably end up with a design consisting of curtain rings taped to the cane and the nylon running through the rings, with a hook tied to on end. Some children may even want to experiment with a float tied to the line somewhere above the hook.

When the children have completed their rods ask them to devise a series of tests so that they are able to judge the strength, mobility and flexibility of their rods.

Try to arrange fishing expeditions for groups of children, so that they can use their rods. It would be advisable, at this stage, to contact a local angling club, especially if it has a junior section, to see if any help would be forthcoming in this direction. Permits are necessary for fishing, so contact the local community police officer for his advice before embarking on the project.

When the children go fishing they should be carefully supervised by adults, and it will probably be as well if the adults remove the hook from the mouths of any fish caught before slipping them back into the water.

Further activity
As the children become more adept and interested in fishing ask them to think of any fishing aids which they may be able to make. They might want to experiment with making supports for their rods out of cleft sticks or learning more about the different kinds of bait available.

23. Bird watching

Age range
Nine to ten.

Group size
Individuals and pairs.

What you need
Notebooks, pencils, binoculars, string, peanuts.

What to do
One of the simplest and most interesting ways of getting children of this age out of the school and into an unfamiliar environment is by taking them on a bird-watching expedition.

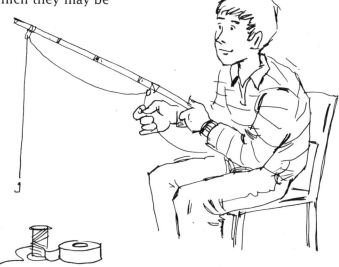

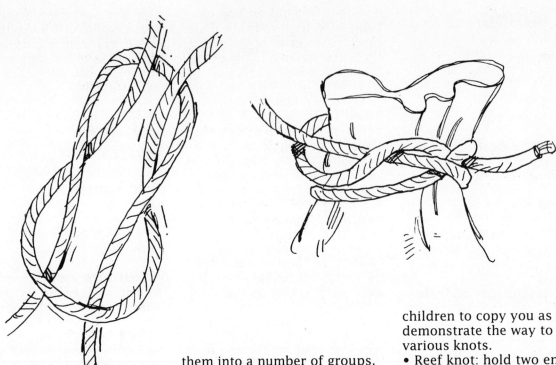

To initially arouse their interest and enthusiasm it will help to develop some form of bird garden in the school grounds, preferably outside the classroom window. Hang peanuts from lines, or scatter food over a bird table and encourage the children to watch and make notes about the birds which visit the garden.

The children should be able to identify the more common bird visitors and there are a number of excellent books which will help them do this, including *The RSPB Guide to Watching British Birds* by D. Saunders (Hamlyn, 1984) and *The Nature Trail Book of Birdwatching* by Malcolm Hart (Usborne, 1976).

When taking the children out on an expedition, split them into a number of groups, each under the supervision of an adult and preferably with a pair of binoculars to pass around the group. Select a wooded area and encourage the children to make notes and sketches of what they see. Ask them to make collections which could be used as a display back in the classroom such as feathers, pellets and so on.

24. Knots

Age range
Nine to ten.

Group size
Pairs and small groups.

What you need
Length of rope or twine, tin cans, sacks or bags.

What to do
Teach the children how to tie a number of basic knots. Give each child a length of thin rope or twine and ask the children to copy you as you demonstrate the way to tie the various knots.
• Reef knot: hold two ends of the same piece of rope. Place the left hand over the right hand and take it over. Then take the right hand back over the left hand and push it through. To use the reef knot to join two ropes, make loops out of each piece of rope. Push one loop into the other and pull the two left hand pieces through.
• Sack knot: place a piece of rope round the top of a sack. Wind the string round and under the first cross-over. This should produce a figure of eight. Carry the rope round the front again, taking it over and then under the rope there. Pull the loose ends of the rope together to close the sack.

Organise the children into pairs and ask them to practise tying and untying these knots. End the session by organising a number of relays. Organise the children in teams of seven or eight and place two ropes so that they are about 40m ahead of each team. On the command 'go', the first child in each team should run to the ropes, join them using a reef knot and run back. The second child must then run up to the ropes and untie them and run back, and so on.

Retaining the same teams, place a sack or paper bag of rubbish and a length of rope or string 40m ahead of each team. The first child in each team must then run to the sack, tie it with a sack knot and run back. The second child must run to the sack, untie it and run back, and so on.

25. Collecting litter

Age range
Nine to ten.

Group size
Pairs.

What you need
Paper sacks, gloves.

What to do
Divide the class into pairs. Give each pair a paper sack and each child a pair of gloves.

For a stated period, say a month, place each pair of children in charge of one area of the school, to collect and dispose of all the litter accumulating there.

Ask the class to draw maps showing the areas for which each pair is responsible. Give points for ingenious ways of collecting litter.

26. Preparing a wild-life pond

Age range
Nine to ten.

Group size
The whole class.

What you need
Spades, plastic sheeting, old carpet, rocks, soil, nets, jars.

What to do
Tell the children that they are going to make a school pond.

Ask them to select a suitable area of unused land in the school and dig a hole. They should then line the hole with the carpet and place the plastic sheeting over the carpet. They should then cover the sheeting with a layer of fine soil.

Go on supervised expeditions to established ponds to find suitable aquatic plants and taking only one plant from each group plant these in the soil of your school pond filling the hole with water.

Go back to the natural ponds and tell the children to dip their nets into the water to find examples of pond life. They can put the insects they find into jars of water and bring them back and place them in the school pond.

27. Estimating time

Age range
Nine to ten.

Group size
Individuals and pairs.

What you need
Pencils, paper, stop-watches.

What to do
Place the children in pairs and give each pair a distance to estimate.

Ask the children to measure the distance by guessing and then by counting how many paces it takes to cross it. How close were they?

Ask each pair to estimate how long it will take them to walk the distance and then to run the distance. Provide each pair with a stop-watch. The first child should then walk the distance while the second child times her. They can then reverse the roles.

Repeat this with a number of different distances. Do the children's estimates become more accurate with practice? Are their estimates more accurate over a shorter distance or a longer one? Why do they think this is?

28. Looking at the countryside

Age range
Nine to ten.

Group size
Individuals and pairs.

What you need
Pencils, paper, stop-watches.

What to do
Take the children on a country walk and ask them to observe and record what they see. Tell them to count the number of flowers in a square metre patch of a field and then estimate the size of the field. They can then use these figures to estimate how many flowers there are in the whole field.

Ask the children to draw the different geometrical shapes they see during the expedition. For example, there may be rectangular gates, square fields and so on.

If the children can find a stream, tell them to throw a twig into the water and measure the time it takes for the stick to cover 10m. Can they work out the speed of the current in the stream from this? If this is too difficult ask them to estimate whether the current is *slow* or *fast*.

29. Constructing a shelter

Age range
Nine to ten.

Group size
Individuals.

What you need
Large stones, sheets.

What to do
When out on an expedition look for a low wall and tell the children to try to construct a shelter using a sheet and a number of large stones. The shelter must provide a roof of sorts, under which the child who has constructed it can sleep.

The children may come up with a variety of ideas, but the basic bivouac is constructed by anchoring one side of the sheet to the top of the wall with a row of large stones, and anchoring the bottom end to the ground at the foot of the wall with another row of stones.

30. Organising room in a tent

Age range
Nine to ten.

Group size
Groups of three and four.

What you need
Small tents, rucksacks, sleeping bags, camping equipment.

What to do
Erect a number of small tents in the school grounds or nearby field. Children of this age may be too young to do this unaided, so the assistance of adults will probably be needed.

Make sure that each child has a rucksack containing basic camping equipment and also a sleeping bag. Divide the children into teams of three or four, according to the size of the tents available. Tell them to imagine that they are on a camping expedition and that they are sharing a tent. You want them to organise the space in the tent, so that their sleeping bags are unrolled and their rucksacks unpacked. The conditions in the tent should be both tidy and hygienic. You can do this as a competition, awarding points for various aspects of the layout.

31. Preparing a camp-fire

Age range
Nine to ten.

Group size
Small groups.

What you need
Bricks, spades, iron grids.

What to do
Find an area where you can practise preparing a camp fire. If there is a spare piece of land attached to the school this would be ideal. Organise the children into teams of six or seven. If the ground is bare, tell each team to dig a shallow pit. If the area is grassy, they should carefully dig out the

turfs and place them in the shade. These should be replaced later. They must then line the sides of the pit with bricks, standing them on their sides, leaving a few centimetres between each one. Tell them to put another layer of bricks on top of the first ones, overlapping the gaps in the first row. This will form a basic fireplace.

Ask the children to gather dry wood and kindling and place these between the bricks. Finally, you should place the iron grid across the top layer of bricks and add any pots ready for cooking!

Further activity
Ask the children to try to design and make a screen which may be sited to keep the wind coming from one direction off the fire.

32. Packing rucksacks

Age range
Nine to ten.

Group size
Individuals.

What you need
Rucksacks and contents such as waterproof clothing, socks, plates, eating utensils, jumpers, gloves, soap, towels and so on.

What to do
Tell the children that you want each of them to pack a rucksack as neatly and sensibly as possible and to carry it over a stipulated route.

Place each child on a starting line with an empty rucksack and a pile of the things which will need to go in it at their feet. They must then pack their rucksacks, so that the things they will need first at the camp site will be at the top of the pack.

Watch the children as they pack and award points for common sense and neatness. As soon as each rucksack is packed the child should put it on and walk as quickly as he can to the finishing line about 100m away. More points can be awarded for the order in which the children finish. The overall winner will be the child who gets the most combined points.

If there is time, the children could also be asked to unpack their rucksacks and pile the contents neatly on the finishing line and more points could be allocated for this.

33. Choosing a camp site

Age range
Nine to ten.

Group size
Small groups.

What you need
Pencils, paper, compasses.

What to do
Take the children out to an area of undulating countryside. Divide them into groups – making sure one adult supervises each group.

Tell the groups that they must explore the surrounding countryside and select the best place they can find for a camp site of about ten tents and 30 children.

Give the children some basic criteria for their choice, such as shelter from the wind and free from obvious dangers, and ask the teams to select their own additional criteria.

Ask the children to make notes and sketches of the areas they choose and, if possible, to give compass references as they explore the area and make their choices.

When you all return to the classroom the children can compile a file about their potential sites, writing up their notes, making fair copies of the maps and so on. Finish this activity with a class discussion on the ways in which the teams arrived at their decisions.

34. Building a dry stone wall

Age range
Nine to ten.

Group size
The whole class.

What you need
Stones of assorted sizes, rubble, soil.

What to do
If the school has access to a sizeable consignment of stones then you can ask the children to construct a dry stone wall, using only the stones themselves.

Tell the children that the wall is to be no more than 1m high. Make sure you select a piece of flat land and ask the children to spread the stones along the complete length of the proposed wall. This will help the children to select the rest of the stones they want.

Tell the class that building their wall is going to be rather like putting a jigsaw puzzle together. For the bottom row they will need the largest, flattest stones. For the second row they should use the remaining large stones. The children should stop and ensure that the wall is not slanting too much to one side and any holes should be filled with soil and rubble, until the stones are steady and secure. Ask them to devise ways of checking that the wall is straight.

As the wall gets higher, smaller and smaller stones will have to be used, except for the top row, which should consist of large stones once more.

NB: In the interests of safety do not make the wall more than 1m high. Make sure that there is adequate adult supervision at each stage.

35. Mini-orienteering

Age range
Ten to eleven.

Group size
Pairs.

What you need
Pencils, paper, maps, coloured bands, photocopiable page 184.

What to do
Orienteering consists of being asked to read a map and following a route to reach a destination. The children can be introduced to a modified form of this on the school premises if they are large enough.

Work out a route for the children and write this out using photocopiable page 184 and duplicate it. Mark on it several check points which the children must report to, and the final destination. This information could look something like this:

```
START
Outside Class 1

CHECK POINTS
(a) door of Boiler House
(b) oak tree in school field
(c) centre spot on football pitch

DESTINATION
Outside Class 8
```

The children might use this information to visualise their route and draw their own sketch map from the list.

Place a number of coloured bands at each check point, so that there is a different colour at each one, and put a number of quoits at the final destination.

The children should work in pairs using their sketch maps of the route to collet one band from each check point and a quoit from the destination. Start each pair so that there is about a minute time lapse between them.

You can repeat this exercise a number of times, using different check points and destinations, and the children can work individually as well as in pairs.

36. Orienteering – counting paces

Age range
Ten to eleven.

Group size
Individuals and pairs.

What you need
Tape measures, trundle wheels, pencils, paper.

What to do

Tell the children that you want them to estimate distances and then measure them to see how close their estimates are. Tell the children that they will be working in pairs in the playground or school field. Show each pair an object placed some distance away and ask the children to estimate how many walking paces they think they are from the object. The children can then check the distance by pacing it out. Who had the closest estimate to the real distance?

You can repeat this exercise by giving each pair a number of different distances to estimate and then check. Ask the children to write down their estimates and then the actual distances they have paced out. When each pair has paced out a distance, ask them to estimate the distance in metres. Again they can check their estimates by using tape measures or trundle wheels.

The children can also estimate distances in *running* steps. They can run the distance in pairs, comparing the distances between them. (A running step is counted every time the left foot strikes the ground.)

Finish this activity with the children working individually. They should choose their own objects, estimating how many paces and running steps there are between them and the objects, and then checking these distances and measuring them.

37. Orienteering: points of the compass

Age range
Ten to eleven.

Group size
Individuals and pairs.

What you need
Compasses, pencils, paper.

What to do
Organise the children into pairs and give each one a compass. Check that they know how to read the main points and then give the

children compass bearings and distances in paces which they are to follow; for example, north 50 paces or south 34 paces. As the children grow more adept, increase the difficulty of the bearings, for example, north-west 31 paces or south-east 27 paces.

Tell the children to work on their own with compasses and to plot routes involving several changes of direction; for example, north 20 metres, then south 30 metres, then west 50 metres and so on. They can then check their routes and see how accurate they were.

38. Orienteering: ground to air signals

Age range
Ten to eleven.

Group size
Individuals and small groups.

What you need
Old clothes, rags, assorted PE apparatus such as benches, skittles and so on.

What to do
Show the children the basic international ground-to-air signals. These signals are marked out on the ground and used when members of

expeditions are in distress and wish to signal to aircraft.
• Y means yes, we need help.
• N means no, we do not need anything
• X means unable to proceed.

Ask each child to use her own body to form the Y signal. She should lie on the ground, so that an aircraft would recognise the signal. Then ask each child to work out and demonstrate with her body the X signal.

Tell the children to work in teams and ask them to devise as many ways as they can of making the Y signal so that it could be seen from quite a height. They could use collections of clothing, assorted pieces of PE apparatus, chairs and other pieces of furniture.

Judge and comment on the various efforts, and then ask the teams to do the same with the X signal.

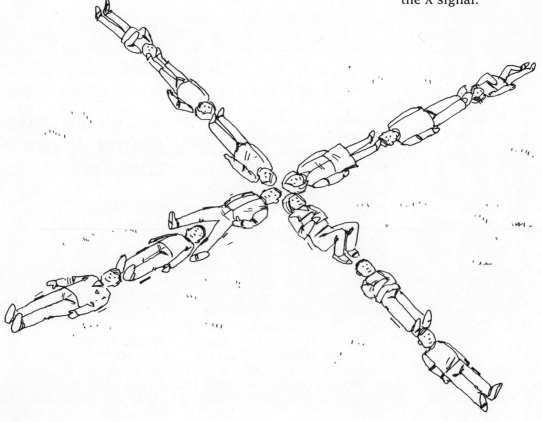

CHAPTER 6

Swimming

The National Curriculum requires that by the end of Key Stage 2 all children are able to swim 25 metres and demonstrate an understanding of water safety. However, it is left to the school to decide whether children will be taught at Key Stage 1 or Key Stage 2, or whether the swimming programme will extend over both these stages.

If the entire swimming provision takes place at Key Stage 1, care must be taken to ensure that the children are still capable of reaching the required standards some years later at the end of Key Stage 2. Another consideration at the planning stage is whether older children may be more capable of grasping the principles of water safety than younger ones.

The aim of this chapter is to provide a graduated series of activities, enjoyable in themselves, which will enable the teacher to meet the requirements of the National Curriculum.

The activities cover the age range across both key stages, but if the swimming programme in your school begins some way in to the age range, you can select those activities suggested for younger children as appropriate.

BACKGROUND

Organisation

As few primary schools possess their own swimming pools, the majority will have to use public swimming pools for swimming lessons. This means that a great deal of the lesson organisation will be undertaken by the pool staff, but the onus will still be with the class teacher to check that certain basic requirements are met to ensure the safety of the children.

The pool

Ideally, a class of learners should have the pool to themselves; if this is not possible the area being used by the learners should be roped off, so that it is under the control of the teacher and her helpers. The water temperature should be around 30°C, and in the early stages, the water should be shallow and you should make sure that the floor of the pool does not slope. It is imperative that no child is allowed to get out of her depth.

Staff

If most of the children in a teaching group cannot swim you should ensure that there are no more than 15 children to each teacher. Wherever possible, the teacher should stand on the side of the pool, where she is in control and can see what is going on. It will be of great help if two or three parents who can actually join the children in the water, to demonstrate strokes and generally help the children.

Time

The actual time the children spend in the water for a swimming session should not usually exceed more than 30 minutes. Most of this pool time should be utilised for allowing the children to move about, rather than standing around the poolside listening to the teacher. A minimum of actual instruction, followed by a great deal of practical help as the children follow instructions, should be the aim of each session.

Discipline

Most children enjoy water activities and it is easy for the noise level in a pool to rise to considerable proportions. It is important to keep the noise level to a minimum and you must insist on utter and complete obedience and discipline from the children when they are in the water and at the side of the pool.

Discipline should start in the changing rooms, with the children changing quickly and quietly and using any foot baths before they file out with the teacher to the side of the pool. Children must *never,* under any circumstances, run along the side of the pool or enter the water without the permission of the teacher or when the teacher is not present. All entry into the water must be supervised. The children should always use the steps leading into the water until they are ready to jump or dive in, again under supervision. There must be no mayhem in the water. The children should not organise their own games or romp around, pushing one another.

Reluctant swimmers

Usually one or two children will be nervous and reluctant to enter the water straightaway. Do not force them in or draw attention to them. Instead, let the reluctant swimmers sit at the side of the pool splashing their feet in the water. As a rule they will join the others before long, but if they seem to be delaying their entry rather too long, try to get one of the 'in the pool' helpers to take the child in to the shallow end on her own.

Safety

As long as there are children in the water the teacher must never leave the pool side. She should always be on the alert for the unexpected and life-saving equipment must be available at the pool. Always have a long pole handy to lower into the water, and push one end towards any child in difficulties. It is a good idea to pair children off, not just for partner activities, but so that they are responsible for one another. One partner should always be aware of what the other is doing, so that an adult can be informed if any emergency should occur.

Take great care to supervise any diving activities when the children become more proficient. Insist on children paying strict attention to instructions during the lesson.

Aids

There are many commercial swimming aids on the market, and some of them are very useful, especially in the learning stages. They give non-swimmers confidence, provide buoyancy and help the children to maintain a horizontal body position while keeping their heads above water and breathing freely. Among the aids which will be of assistance are:
• arm bands;
• body rings;
• floats;
• kickboards;
• rubber diving bricks;
• weighted hoops;
• diving sticks;
• discs which flutter to the bottom of the pool.

When fitting buoyancy aids to children, take time to check that they work properly and that they fit correctly. As soon as a child seems confident enough to discard such aids allow her to do so.

ACTIVITIES

Water familiarisation

The following introductory activities are intended to help children to gain confidence in water. All these activities should be carried out in a learner pool or in the shallow end of the main pool.

At the end of the second activity and most subsequent sessions, help individual children to use and then discard the various buoyancy aids which they may be using. Arm floats are very useful in the initial stages when children are learning elementary strokes and movements. It is important to judge the right moment to lessen the dependency of

children on arm floats. Gradually deflate the floats as children grow more adept and confident, until they can do without them altogether. Children will develop confidence at different rates. Some will be able to do without floats very quickly, while others will want to retain them for some time.

Floats are the buoyant boards to which children can cling while pushing themselves across the water. Again, the children should be weaned away gradually from their use. At first the children will rely considerably on their support. Encourage the child to use less and less of the float, until he is resting only his finger tips on it, and then doing without the help of the float altogether.

Rings give children added security, but should be deflated centimetre by centimetre, until the child can manage without the ring.

1. Introduction to the water

Age range
Five to six.

Group size
Individuals or pairs.

What you need
Arm bands, rubber rings.

What to do
Encourage the children to climb down into the water. They should take their time and hold on to the rail with both hands while facing the side of the pool. Make sure that there is an adequate amount of space between each child.

Once the children are in the water, ask them to imagine that they are soldiers marching

on the spot. Retaining their grip on the rail, they should lift and replace their feet in their own time, pausing for a rest now and again. Praise the children who are lifting their knees really high.

Let the class continue with this for three or four minutes, encouraging them all the time. Then, bring them to a halt and ask them to release their hold on the rail with one hand, but retaining their grip with the other. Ask them to pull their free hands through the water in as many directions as possible – forwards, backwards, up and down, behind the back and so on. After a few minutes the children can then start splashing the water with their free hands.

Make sure that you watch out for timid children who may become a little apprehensive once the class start splashing. If necessary, move them so that they are a little distance from the more boisterous children. This way the more timid children should slowly gain in confidence and will probably ask to rejoin the others.

Throughout the lesson the children can change their gripping hands but they must always maintain a hold on the rail in these early confidence-building stages.

Change the activities throughout the time available. Tell the children to lift one leg at a time and to move it in as many directions through the water as they can, moving it slowly, shaking it and then kicking. Tell them to move their whole bodies in as many ways as they can – shaking, bobbing, shivering, swaying, twisting and so on.

Towards the end of the lesson, let the children work in pairs to devise more movements of their bodies. They can work individually or together with a partner, but must still hold on to the rail with one hand.

Finally, you can allow the children to let go of the rail, select a space and carry out any of the activities they have practised earlier.

End the session with a game of 'merry-go-round'. Divide the group in half and tell one group to form a circle in the water, standing face inwards, while the remaining children stand behind one of the children in the circle. At the command 'go' the children in the outer ring must walk as quickly as they can in a clockwise direction until they are standing behind their partners again with their hands resting on the shoulders of the children in front. The first child to complete the circuit is the winner. Repeat this game several times, moving both clockwise and anticlockwise alternately, with children in the outer circle changing places with those in the inner circle, and then changing back again.

Further activity

If the pool has the facilities the children should be allowed, under supervision, to use any slides into the water.

2. Moving through water

Age range
Five to six.

Group size
Individuals.

What you need
Arm bands, rubber rings.

What to do
Work with the children until they can walk comfortably through the water, taking their feet off the bottom of the pool for short periods. Ask them to walk round the shallow area, changing direction when you tell them to – left, right, backwards, sideways, forwards and so on. The children can then try moving by sliding their feet over the floor of the pool, hopping first on one leg and then on the other.

Finally, they can try walking with bent knees, keeping their shoulders submerged and their chins as close to the surface of the water as possible.

Try to persuade the children to take their feet off the floor of the pool for a few seconds at a time. They should adopt a crouching position in the water – knees bent, shoulders submerged, chins resting on the water – and take one foot off the bottom. They should then take their other foot off the bottom, so that their bodies float for a second or two.

Give the children plenty of practice, encouraging them to raise their feet higher and higher, until their knees almost reach their chins. Ask them to experiment with their arm movements too. Some children should end up in a sitting position in the water, with their arms extended and knees well up. These children can then show the others what they are doing and how they achieved it.

Further activities
When most children can achieve the sitting position in the water with their arms extended, they should progress to practising some sort of pulling movement as a preamble to a rudimentary swimming stroke. Show the children a basic dog paddle, pulling both arms at the same time through the water. Ask them to practise this and to experiment with other pulling movements, using one hand or two in a variety of ways.

3. Early water games

Age range
Five to six.

Group size
Individuals or small groups.

What you need
Arm bands, rubber rings, hoops.

What to do
Encourage the children to feel at home in the water. Let them move about in it freely and immerse as much of their bodies as possible.

Ask the children to line up behind a leader, each child placing her hands on the shoulders of the child in front. The children can then play a game of 'follow-the-leader'. Tell the leading child to change direction frequently so that the other children have to try hard to maintain their grips and keep up with him. After they have had a number of practice attempts, any child who cannot maintain a hold on the child in front is out.

From time to time shout 'change' When you do this the children should stop and turn. The last child in the line then becomes the leader and continues with the game.

After about 10 minutes, stop the children and tell them to change their grip on the children in front (for example, holding around the waist, placing a hand on her head

and so on). This will also give you a chance to quieten them down.

Usually, the children become so engrossed in this game that they forget any fears they may have of the water. When all the children seem confident, add another factor to the game. Tell them to imagine that the line they are forming is really a ship and when you call 'abandon ship' they must abandon the vessel by throwing themselves over the side into the water. Many children will throw themselves into the water freely. Others will be more cautious. Do not draw attention to the more inhibited children as they will gain confidence as they become familiar with the game.

Further activities

Ask the children to sit in the shallow water with their arms extended behind them, leaning backwards and taking their weight on their hands. If they splash their feet vigorously, their bottoms may lift a little, allowing the children to experience buoyancy. By

allowing their heads to fall back until their ears are immersed in water, the children may even move backwards a little if they continue to thresh with their legs.

Put the children in groups of four or five and tell them to play 'ring a ring o' roses'. They should join hands in a circle and walk or skip round as they sing. On the word 'down', the children should bob down into the water. Allow them to bow down as far as they feel comfortable, but they should gradually immerse themselves deeper and deeper as they gain experience and confidence.

Finally, float a hoop on top of the water and ask the children to bob down beneath the surface and come up somewhere inside the hoop. As they grow more proficient, ask them to see how long they can remain beneath the surface before coming up inside the hoop.

4. Placing the face in the water

Age range
Five to six.

Group size
Individuals.

What you need
Arm bands, rubber rings.

What to do
Ask the children to kneel in the shallow water, with their hands on the bottom of the pool. Tell them to look into the water and call out what they can see – such as the pattern on the floor of the pool. Encourage them to place their faces into the water and blow gently at the same time. Most children will take their faces out of the water almost

immediately, but encourage them to put them back into the water, increasing the length of time on each occassion. Remind them to keep blowing as they do so. The objective is to get the children to blow into the water with their faces submerged for up to 30 seconds.

Once all the children have managed to submerge their faces for at least a few seconds, gather them all at the side of the pool and ask them to tell you what they have done and what it felt like. Praise the ones who are showing confidence and encourage those who are still finding it difficult.

Ask the children to adopt the kneeling position in the water again and ask them to continue blowing. When most of them seem to be performing the exercise with little difficulty, start timing them out loud. Give the class a signal to submerge their faces and then count loudly from one to ten. See how many of the children can keep their faces beneath the water for ten seconds. Allow the children a further few minutes of free practice.

Further activities

When the children are able to support themselves on their hands or hands and knees with their faces submerged, encourage them to crawl forward while still blowing into the water. Suggest that they change direction as often as they can, while keeping their faces submerged for as long as is comfortable.

Ask the children to sit or squat in shallow water, with their faces beneath the surface. Encourage them to open their eyes and blow out, watching the bubbles rise to the surface. Gradually increase the period of time they spend beneath the surface with their eyes open.

End this session with a game of bobbing up and down. In their own time, let the children bob down beneath the surface in a squatting position with their eyes open and come back to the surface straight away. Encourage the children to increase the number of bobs they make in a minute.

5. Opening eyes under water

Age range
Five to six.

Group size
Individuals, small groups or pairs.

What you need
Arm bands, rubber rings, weights, sinkers, weighted hoops, stop-watch.

What to do
Allow the children to repeat the kneeling exercise in shallow water (see the previous activity), placing their faces in the water and blowing gently. Ask them to open their eyes briefly to see the bubbles rising. Encourage them to repeat this exercise for as long as is comfortable, opening their eyes to watch the bubbles for increasing periods of time.

Give a signal for the children to crawl around in the water on their hands and knees, with their faces in the water. Ask them to keep opening their eyes so that they can see where they are going.

Turn this into a game by putting the children into groups of four, each under the supervision of an adult. Start each group crawling around its own allocated section of the pool. The children should keep their eyes open for as long as possible. Time each group with a stop-watch to see how long they can move without bumping into one another. See how many groups can last a minute without having any underwater collisions.

Children may find great difficulty in opening their eyes under water for a sustained period of time at first, so be prepared to extend these activities over a number of sessions. If this is included as an integral part of a number of enjoyable games, it will eventually become second nature to them.

Ask the children to choose partners and stand opposite sides of the pool from each other. One child in each pair must then crawl across the width of the pool towards their partners. Give marks to each child who plots an accurate course and ends up touching their partner's legs.

Elaborate upon this idea by putting the children into groups of three. One child in each group must then crawl across the pool from one side to the other, with her face in the water. The second child should stand half-way across the pool, with his legs apart, while the third child should stand against the far side of the pool. When you tell the first child to 'go' she must start crawling across the pool through the legs of the child standing in the middle and end up by touching the legs of the child standing against the side of the pool.

Each child should take it in turn to be the one crawling across the pool. As the children gain confidence, organise a series of races between groups. However, it is important to remain alert and make sure that the children who are crawling do not raise their heads to see where they are going. They must open their eyes under water.

Further activities

As the children gain in confidence and have no trouble opening their eyes under water there are many other activities which they could do.

Place a number of rubber diving bricks on the floor of the pool and give each child one minute to go to the bottom, find the bricks and bring as many as possible to the surface in the time allowed.

You may also use commercial sinkers which sink to the bottom of the pool slowly. These may be used to help children who are still unsure about keeping their eyes open under water. As the sinkers float gently down the children should be able to retrieve them without keeping their eyes open for too long.

Hoops may also be used to give the children general confidence and enable them to use their eyes under water. Leave a hoop to float on the surface and ask the children to crawl and then stand up in the centre of the hoop. This could be carried out as a relay race,

with the children crawling along the bottom of the pool and coming to the surface through a number of hoops placed across the width of the pool. There are also available specially designed hoops which stand in an upright position in the water. Use these for relay races, with the children crawling through several of these hoops while keeping their faces immersed in the water and their eyes open.

Also, encourage the children to lie face downwards in shallow water, supporting themselves on their hands and leaving their legs trailing. They can then start bobbing their faces in and out of the water, keeping their eyes open and concentrating on breathing as their faces come out of the water.

Finally, end with a game of 'I see you' where one child stands in front of the other children who stand scattered about the pool behind him. The child in front should face away from the others, but at frequent, irregular intervals he should spin round and face them; as he does this the other children must bob beneath the surface. If he sees any heads still above the surface, then these children go to the front and become 'spotters' as well.

6. Water games with balls

Age range
Five to six.

Group size
Individuals, pairs and small groups.

What you need
Arm bands, rubber rings, balls of different sizes.

What to do
Start this activity by giving each child a ball and asking the children to throw them across the water, follow them and retrieve them. Continue by placing the children in pairs and asking them to throw a ball to one another. As they grow more proficient, increase the distance between the children. Any child who does not catch the ball must retrieve it so that the game may continue.

Place the children in threes so that one child stands between the other two, and let them continue the throwing game. It is the middle child's task to intercept the ball as the others throw it to one another. If he does so, then the last child to throw the ball takes his place in the middle.

Give each child a ball again and ask the class to move their balls across the pool while they walk, using as many different parts of their body as they can to manipulate them. Once they reach the other side they should balance the ball, using as many different parts of their bodies as they can think of. The children can then work in pairs to think of ways of moving the balls and then balancing them.

End this session with a relay race. The first child in each team must propel a ball across the width of the pool in any way they choose, but making sure that the ball is never more than half a metre from their bodies. Once they reach the far side they must turn and come back, handing the ball to the next child in their team, who sets out in turn.

Further activity
This would be an appropriate stage to ask the children to experiment with different ways of entering the water. Depending upon how confident individual children are, these methods could range from walking down the steps to sitting on the side and slipping in to the water, or stepping in from the side of the pool, and even jumping in.

Feet off the bottom

It will assist the confidence of the children if they learn to move through the water in some fashion as soon as possible. Keep a close eye on the children's needs and vary the depth of water according to their different stages of development. However, it is important to make sure that they are always in their own depth.

1. Floating and moving

Age range
Five to six.

Group size
Individuals or pairs.

What you need
Arm bands, rubber rings.

What to do
Before teaching the class the components of basic strokes, provide them with a number of opportunities to move through the water. Ask the children to kneel on their hands and knees in water which allows their faces to be above the surface while they are kneeling. Tell them to put all their weight on to their palms and at the same time push back their feet and extend their legs. Tell them to trail their legs and 'walk' forward on their hands. Allow them plenty of time to move around in this fashion, stopping to rest when they want to.

When they have grown accustomed to the movement, suggest that every so often they go up on to their fingertips and then pull their hands up off the floor for a few seconds at a time. If they

do this, they will soon find themselves floating. Some of the more adventurous and confident among the children may also be able to maintain this floating position for quite appreciable periods of time.

Tell the children that they have been floating, and that the next stage from this is to move themselves through the water by swimming a few strokes. Ask them to adopt one of the floating positions they have practised in an earlier lesson. They should crouch in the water with their shoulders submerged and draw their knees up to their chests, taking their feet off the bottom of the pool. They should then extend their arms sideways until they are floating. They must pull their arms through the water rapidly in a dog paddle. If at the same time they can splash behind them with their feet they may find that they are moving through the water.

To end the session, the children could be placed in pairs and asked to help each

other to devise and practise ways of moving through the water.

Further activity
Introduce the children to other methods of floating and encourage them to practise these in further sessions.
• The 'jellyfish' float – the children should stand waist-deep in water, breathe and stoop to touch their ankles, immersing their heads in the water. They should keep their legs as straight as possible and take their feet off the ground, allowing their bottoms and backs to rise to the surface. They should hold their breath and maintain the position for as long as possible, before dropping their feet to the floor and standing up.
• The 'turtle' float – the children should stand in the water up to their chins and then drop their heads forward

into the water and allow their arms to drift forward. They should then bend their knees and lift their feet off the bottom and float suspended in this fashion. To stand up again, tell the children to drop their feet back on to the floor.

2. Gliding through water

Age range
Five to six.

Group size
Individuals and pairs.

What you need
Arm bands, rubber rings.

What to do
Use the children's new-found confidence to start them gliding face-down through the water. Ask each child to stand at the rail with a partner. One child in each pair should face and grasp the rail, and at a signal from you, raise one leg backwards. His partner should then support him as he raises his second leg, so that both legs are extended just under the surface of the water. Allow the children to swap roles a number of times until the whole class has experienced grasping the rail and extending their legs.

Next, ask all the children to face the side of the pool and submerge their shoulders. Ask them to take one step back and extend both hands in front of them. At a signal from you, ask them to push forward smoothly, reach the bar, hold it and then stand up.

Keep repeating this exercise until most of the children can perform it unhurriedly and with confidence. Make sure that the children place their faces in the water as they go forward and then gradually increase the distance between the children and the rail, according to the competence of each child.

Finally, organise the children into pairs and ask each child to push away from the wall towards her partner, using the impetus of the push to glide as far as possible. Her partner should receive her and assist her to stand. Tell the receiving children to stand further away from their partner and make sure all children glide and receive.

Further activity
Hold races to see which child can glide farthest from the wall using one leg to push against it.

Hold a 'chariot race' where one child in a pair adopts the prone position – lying with his face in the water and his hands extended ahead. The other child should face her partner and grasp his hands. On the command from you the standing child should start to walk backwards, towing the other child in a prone position to the other side of the pool. Once at his end the children should exchange positions and move back to the other side of the pool in the same way.

You could also allow the children to practise the glide, concentrating on establishing a streamlined position. This may be attained by the child lying on his stomach and extending both hands and arms before him. He should grasp the thumb of the other hand and keep his ankles together as he glides.

3. Leg kick for front crawl

Age range
Five to six.

Group size
Individuals and pairs.

What you need
Arm bands, rubber rings, floats.

What to do

Begin this session by letting the children repeat some of the gliding exercises they performed in the previous activity. After a while, stop them and ask them to think about what has stopped them from gliding even further than they have already done. Tell them that you want them to perform one more glide, and to work out in their minds what brought them to a halt.

When the children have completed the final glide, bring them to the side again and repeat the question. With luck, one or two children will say that their legs seemed to get heavy and sink, bringing the glide to a conclusion. If no one comes up with this suggestion, ask one of the children to perform a glide while everyone else watches her legs. Tell the class that if they can add a 'kick' to their glide it will take them even further and bring them ever closer to the act of swimming.

Line the children up against the rail, facing the side of the pool. Demonstrate the kick stroke for the front crawl. To do this correctly the child should be in a prone position with her face in the water. The kick should begin from her hips and she should try to avoid bending her knees too much.

Allow the children to practise the kick while holding on to the rail. This is a tiring exercise and the children should be given plenty of opportunities to rest. When some of them seem to be getting the idea, move on to performing the kick while holding on to a float. Do not worry if the children seem to be using up too much energy at this stage. Relaxation will come with confidence. Some of

the children will make appreciable progress as they move about the pool. Tell them to experiment with different positions and grips as they manipulate their floats placing them under the body, using them to support the chin holding them forward at arm's length and so on.

4. Combining arm and leg strokes

Age range
Five to six.

Group size
Individuals.

What you need
Arm bands, rubber rings.

What to do
By now many children will be impatient to start swimming, if they have not already made their first tentative efforts to do so. Do not expect technical perfection at this stage. Once the children have started

swimming with reasonable confidence it should be quite easy to develop the finer points of the various strokes later.

Start by telling the children to adopt the floating position, squatting in shallow water with their knees drawn up under their chins and their arms extended sideways for balance. Ask them to start moving forward by pulling their arms through the water in the dog paddle.

Allow the children to practise this for some time, encouraging and helping them, before calling them to the side of the pool to demonstrate the next movement. Remind them of the leg movement for the front crawl. Ask them to hold the rail and let their legs trail out behind and then practise threshing their legs up and down together in the front crawl movement. Check the movement of individual children and make any necessary adjustments.

Stop the children and tell them that for the first time they are going to put together arm and leg movements in order to swim. Tell them that for the rest of the period you want them to practise the dog paddle with their arms and at the same time to thresh their legs up and down in the front crawl movement.

Let the children move around the shallow end of the pool, first practising the arm stroke and then the leg stroke, and then encourage them to put both movements together. If there is time at the end of the session hold races between children of roughly similar ability across the width of the pool.

Further activity
As time progresses, encourage the children to increase the scope of their dog paddle

stroke so that their arms are stretched farther and farther ahead of them. Eventually, the more proficient among them will start to break the surface of the water with their arms as they paddle. This may be used at a later stage as the basis for work on the arm stroke of the front crawl.

If all the children are beginning to move freely about the water this would be an appropriate time to remind them of the basic safety precautions.
• unless they are working in pairs they should allow one another plenty of room.
• there should be no horseplay like 'ducking' in the water.
• the children should always be on the alert for any other children in difficulties, in which case an adult should be informed at once.

These safety regulations should be brought home to the children at regular intervals at all ages.

5. Floating on the back

Age range
Six to seven.

Group size
Individuals and pairs.

What you need
Arm bands, rubber rings, small objects such as weighted rings and sinkers.

What to do
If the children have been practising regularly, a number of them should be ready to discard their arm bands and rings. Do not attempt to hurry this process and if a child prefers to retain buoyancy aids let him do so. Similarly, you may decide to increase the depth of water in which certain children are allowed to work.

Begin the session by asking the children to float on their faces with their eyes open and blowing gently into the water. How long can they float like this? Scatter a few small objects on the floor of the pool and ask the children to identify them. Give each child one minute in which to retrieve as many of the objects as possible.

The children can now move on to floating on their backs. This is not always an easy manoeuvre for young children; a supine position should be adopted in the water, with the face clear of the water. Tell the children that in order to maintain this position it may be necessary to make gentle sculling movements with their hands, which should be placed palms downwards at a comfortable angle from the body.

Place the children into pairs and ask one child to float on his back while the other supports him. The supporter should have her hands in position below the body of the floater and should be ready to help the floater adopt a standing position whenever necessary. Make sure the children swap roles so that both have a chance to float and support. Check the positions of each child as they work. The floater should lie straight with his hips, knees and toes on the surface, as well as his face.

See how many children can float unaided in this manner by the end of the session. It will probably be necessary for two or three further sessions to be devoted to this technique of floating.

6. Floating on the back – different positions

Age range
Six to seven.

Group size
Individuals and pairs.

What you need
Arm bands, rubber rings.

What to do
Once the children have mastered the basic technique of floating on their backs, they can increase their confidence and develop more awareness of the water and their own bodies by seeking to adopt different positions as they float. Start off by asking the children to use rings, floats and other buoyancy aids to help them devise and demonstrate different floating positions – on their backs, fronts, crouching, vertical floating and so on. See if they

can think of names for their positions such as stars, letters, fish, circles and so on.

Ask the children who do not normally use aids to discard them, and then organise the children into pairs and ask them to float on their backs, with one child supported by the other. Can they think of names for the positions they are creating in the water?

Finally, ask the children to work on their own, floating on their backs and adopting as many different positions as they can. Give them plenty of time to put their feet on the floor and rest between movements. Let the children show each other some of the more ingenious positions adopted. Try to encourage as many different positions as you can; for example:
• both arms and legs extended in star shape;
• streamlined shape with the arms by the sides;
• streamlined shape with the arms extended beyond the heads and the fingers touching;

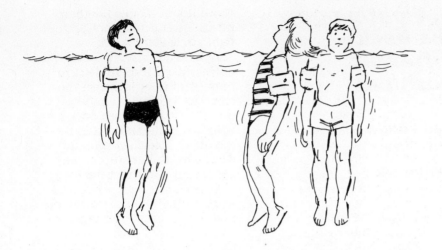

• arms by their sides, one leg extended and the other leg pulled up to the body;
• both arms drawn up and extended and touching above the head;
• legs straight and one arm extended sideways;
• legs straight and one arm curled above the head;
• legs straight with the arms akimbo.

Further activity
Those children who are making good progress could work in small groups devising patterns involving all the children in the group – rather like skydivers changing formation in mid-air. Among the patterns they could form are:
• floating on their backs in circles while extending and touching their hands;
• floating on their backs in a circle with their feet touching;
• floating on their backs in a straight line, like a row of dominoes;
• forming geometrical patterns – squares, circles, rectangles and so on.

7. Other floating positions

Age range
Six to seven.

Group size
Individuals and pairs.

What you need
Arm bands, rubber rings.

What to do
Allow the children to practise floating on their faces and then on their backs, demonstrating different positions. Suggest that they control their movements by using their hands, making sculling motions. Having practised this, call the children to the side of the pool and teach them some of the other basic floating positions.
• Ask the children to adopt a vertical position in the water so that their toes are off the ground. Tell them to place their arms by their sides and tilt back their heads so that their noses and mouths are above the surface. Encourage them to relax and breathe deeply throughout this exercise. When they have

grown accustomed to this position, encourage them to use their hands to spin themselves round in a clockwise and then anticlockwise direction.
• Ask the children to float on their faces and then tuck themselves together, leaning forward. They should rest their chins on their chests and draw their knees up towards their chests, lightly holding their shins to maintain a crouched position. If they inflate their lungs before toppling forwards into this position they should be able to maintain it comfortably in the water.

Allow the children plenty of time to practise the vertical and tuck float, letting them rest their feet on the bottom of the pool as often as they wish. If some children prefer, allow them to help one another adopt and maintain the different positions.

8. Floating as an aid to breathing in the water

Age range
Six to seven.

Group size
Individuals.

What you need
Arm bands, rubber rings.

What to do
The ability of children to breathe as they swim will be enhanced considerably if they are given the opportunity to practise breathing as they float with their faces in the water.

Ask the children to float face down blowing into the water until bubbles are produced. Almost automatically, from time to time, they will raise their faces in order to inhale, before replacing them in the water and blowing bubbles once more.

At a later stage this action can be developed, so that the child inhales as she is lifted out of the water in the process of a swimming stroke.

9. Developing a backstroke kick

Age range
Six to seven.

Group size
Individuals and small groups.

What you need
Arm bands, rubber rings, rubber bricks.

What to do
As a step forward from floating on their backs the children can progress to moving on their backs using the backstroke kick. At a very basic level, this kick consists of the child lying on her back in a streamlined position with her ears just submerged. To kick, she should move each leg alternately, as in the front crawl. She should point her toe as she kicks her first leg up to the surface, making sure her knees are slightly bent. The other leg is kicked downwards to a depth of about half a metre and as the first leg comes down the other leg is brought upwards, and so on.

Allow the children to practise this movement on their own for a time. Then let them work in pairs, so that one child is supporting the other as he lies on his back and does the leg movements.

When the children seem to have mastered the basic leg movement, give each child a rubber brick and tell them to hold the bricks by crossing both arms across their chests. Tell the children to swim on their backs, but using only leg movements. They will be unable to use their arms because these will be supporting the bricks.

Organise individual races between the children while holding the bricks, and then end the session by dividing the class into a number of teams and conducting a relay race across the width of the pool. Each child in each team must carry a brick across the pool, swimming on his back and using the proper leg stroke.

Further activity
If the children show proficiency in swimming with the bricks they could progress to relay races in which each child holds a float to her chest. This could be increased to two floats as the children become more competent at swimming on their backs.

10. Developing a backstroke arm action

Age range
Six to seven.

Group size
Individuals and pairs.

What you need
Arm bands, rubber rings.

What to do
Start by allowing the children to practise the backstroke leg action, first with a partner and then by themselves. You can then teach the backstroke arm action. As a rule, children take to this stroke quite easily as their faces are out of the water and they suffer no problems with confidence.

Point out that in this stroke the arms are always working, rather like the paddles on a vessel churning through the water. As one arm comes out of the water at the completion of a stroke, the other arm is beginning its stroke. To do the backstroke properly, the leading hand should enter the water sideways, so that the little finger breaks the surface. Tell the child to keep her arm as straight as possible. When her hand enters the water she should start pulling at once, keeping her wrist firm and steady for added power. She should carry it through in a sweep, ending the stroke by her thigh. She should lift her arm clear of the water, over her shoulder in a semi-circle and start the next stroke when the other arm emerges from the water.

Allow the children to practise this arm action, first supported by a partner and then on their own. Let them work out their own breathing patterns at this stage.

End the session by asking the children to hook their legs under the rail at the side of the pool. They should then concentrate on the timing of their arm actions, making sure that as one arm enters the water, the other is emerging.

11. Combining backstroke arm and leg actions

Age range
Six to seven.

Group size
Individuals and pairs.

What you need
Arm bands, rubber rings.

What to do
Allow the children, individually and in pairs, to practise separately their backstroke arm and leg actions. Then call them together and teach them how to combine the actions.

Tell them to keep their bodies streamlined and their heads well back. They should start by swimming on their backs using the leg kick only. They can then add the arm stroke to the leg action. It will take a little time to combine

the two actions, but the children should be able to grasp the technique by the end of the session. Encourage them to try and accomplish six leg kicks to each full arm action.

Further activity
Organise games and activities in which the children can use the backstroke. They could take part in relay races in which each child has to propel a balloon through the water to a partner, using their heads to keep it under control while swimming the backstroke. From this they could move on to using only the leg action while placing their hands on their hips.

12. Developing arm movement for front crawl

Age range
Six to seven.

Group size
Individuals and pairs.

What you need
Arm bands, rubber rings.

What to do
When the children have mastered the basic arm and leg actions of the backstroke,

they should have gained enough confidence to return to the basic over-arm stroke they practised earlier (see page 143), and therefore possess the ability to develop the front crawl arm movement.

Allow the children to revise the combined front crawl leg action and dog paddle arm action they have been taught. Remind them to extend the grasp of the arm action, so that they are approaching the movement necessary for basic front crawl.

You can then teach and demonstrate the proper arm action necessary for front crawl. To do this properly the child should stand waist-deep in the water with one foot slightly in front of the other. He should bend forward slightly and extend his right arm forward with his hand slightly cupped and in line with his right eye. His left hand should be positioned by the thigh. He should plunge his right hand in, scooping it through the water until it

reaches his thigh, then taking it out of the water. At the same time he should carry forward his left hand, so that it is placed just as the right hand was before it entered the water. The left hand should then enter the water just as the right hand comes out, ensuring a continuous arm movement.

Supervise the children as they practise this stroke while standing in the water. They can then work in pairs, with one child supporting the other.

End the session by allowing the children to practise the arm action on their own, allowing their legs to dangle behind them. Some children will automatically adopt the correct leg action as well, but do not insist on this to begin with. If the children are fairly competent, let them play a few relay races across the width of the pool, using the arm action for front crawl.

13. Combining the arm and leg actions for front crawl

Age range
Six to seven.

Group size
Individuals.

What you need
Arm bands, rubber rings.

What to do
Allow the children to practise freely, using the dog paddle arm action and the front crawl leg action. Then teach and demonstrate the combined arm and leg actions for the front crawl.

Tell them to push off from the side of the pool and glide in a streamlined position before starting the leg action. Suggest they keep the action fairly shallow, starting it from their hips. They can maintain their balance by using the dog paddle action. They should then change their arm action into the front crawl, kicking their legs at the same time. Show the children that as their arms come out of the water upon the completion of the movement, their heads and bodies turn automatically to one side, providing a good opportunity to take in a deep breath.

Allow the children plenty of time to practise this movement, using two or three sessions if necessary. End each session with relay races using both the leg and arm movements.

14. Games involving front crawl

Age range
Six to seven.

Group size
Small groups.

What you need
Arm bands, rubber rings.

What to do
Begin by telling the children that they are going to improve their style and increase the distance they can swim using the front crawl. Organise a number of relay races involving the use of the front crawl and divide the children into teams to swim the width of the pool.

• Nose-push: ask each child to push a float or inflated balloon ahead of her while swimming, two widths of the pool. She should then hand it over to the next child in the team.

• Towing: divide each team into pairs and ask one child to stand upright while the other clasps him around the waist, legs trailing. On the command to start, the upright child must walk across the pool while the child being towed does the front crawl action. On reaching the other side of the pool, the two children must change position and go back across the pool to the next pair.

•Blind racing: split each team so that half is situated on opposite sides of the pool. The first swimmer in each team is then blindfolded and must set off across the pool, guided to the other side by the shouts of her team-mates. She must touch the next team-mate on the other side before that child can set off back to the next waiting child, and so on.

• Arm-race: let each child complete one width using the front crawl arm stroke only, while trailing his legs behind him.

15. Games involving backstroke

Age range
Six to seven.

Group size
Small groups.

What you need
Arm bands, rubber rings.

What to do
Divide the children into teams and play games which involve the use of the backstroke movements. Make sure that even when the children are enjoying themselves they maintain good style in all the component parts of the stoke they are employing.
• Towing: divide the children into pairs so that one child stands facing the other child who floats on his back. The child who is standing should tow her partner by her heels across the width of the pool, while he does the arm movement for the back crawl. Upon reaching the far side, the two children should change positions and go back across the pool to the next waiting pair in their team.
• Head-push: ask each child in turn to swim a width of the pool using the backstroke and propelling a float or inflated balloon with his head. On reaching the far side he should turn and push the balloon or float back to the next child in his team.
• Leg-race: ask each child in the team to swim two widths of the pool using the leg stroke only, and then hand over to the next child in her team.
• Changing strokes: ask each child in the team to swim one width using the front crawl and then swim back using the backstroke.
• Balance: tell each child in the team to swim two widths using the backstroke while balancing a float on his chest or stomach.

Swimming without aids

If the children have progressed through most of the previous activities they should now be ready to discard their floats, arm bands and rings and take part in an increasing range of water activities.

1. Underwater diving through hoops

Age range
Seven to eight.

Group size
Individuals, pairs and small groups.

What you need
Hoops, diving bricks, string.

What to do
Organise the children into pairs with one child in each pair standing with his legs apart. The other child should stand in the water and then plunge her head into the water, diving to the bottom of the pool and swimming through her partner's legs. She should come up to the surface behind the standing child. Allow them to practise this movement for some time, swapping over roles.

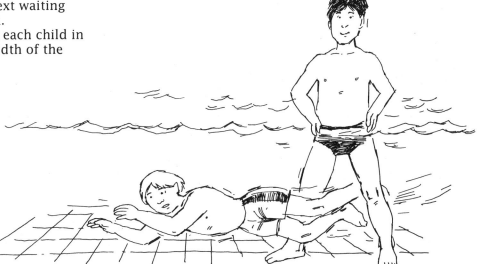

Elaborate on this activity by tying hoops to bricks and placing them on the bottom of the pool. The children should then practise swimming through these hoops. Scatter them about and see how many hoops each child can swim through before coming to the surface for air.

End the session with a relay race. Divide the class into teams and ask half of each team to stand on one side of the pool and the other half on the other side. Secure a hoop to a brick and place it on the floor of the pool so that it is half way across the width of the pool. Give the first child in each team a brick and on the command 'go' this child must swim to the hoop, carrying the brick, and dive through the hoop, placing the brick on the floor by the hoop. He should then surface and continue to swim to the far side of the pool touching the next child in his team. This child then swims to the middle of the pool, dives to pick up the brick, goes through the hoop, surfaces and swims with the brick to the third child. She should hand over the brick and the race continues.

Further activity

Organise the children into pairs and give each pair a small weight to carry. On your command the children must dive into the water from a standing position, swim towards one another, exchange weights under water, swim past one another and then come up to the surface.

2. Pushing a brick underwater

Age range
Seven to eight.

Group size
Individuals and small groups.

What you need
Rubber bricks.

What to do
Give each child a brick and ask the class to place the bricks on the floor of the pool. They must then dive and push the bricks as far as they can along the floor. How far can each child push the brick without surfacing? How far can each child push a brick when coming up for air and then diving again?

Divide the class into teams so that half of each team is on one side of the pool and the other half on the other side. Give the leader of each team a brick and tell him to place it on the floor of the pool. On the order to begin, the leader of each team should submerge and swim along the bottom, pushing the brick ahead of him using any part of his body. When he has placed the brick against the far wall, the second child in his team must dive and push the brick back to the other side of the pool and so on.

Allow the children to surface as many times as necessary while pushing the brick, but make sure that the brick stays on the floor of the pool when the child comes up for air.

NB: It is important that you watch all the children carefully to ensure that they do not wander out of their depth while swimming along the bottom of the pool.

Further activity
Give each child in the team a brick. Tell them to dive to the bottom of the pool, one at a time, and make a pattern on the floor. Judge each pattern for ingenuity.

Conduct an underwater relay race across the pool with the children carrying bricks and passing them on to one another. Allow the children to surface for air whenever they want to.

3. Retrieving coins

Age range
Seven to eight.

Group size
Individuals and small groups.

What you need
Coins.

What to do
Tell the children that you want to see how quickly they can locate and retrieve coins when placed on the floor of the pool. Scatter some coins and allow the children to locate them, bring them to the surface and place them on the side.

Next, organise the children into teams of four and place eight coins on the floor of the pool by each team. Tell the children that all members of the team should dive together, but each child may only bring up one coin at a time. The winning team is the one which

has placed all eight coins on the side of the pool first.

Play this game four or five times and then increase the number of coins to ten and then to twelve, placing them over a wider area of the pool each time. Make certain that the children keep their eyes open when under the water and searching for the coins.

4. Water tag

Age range
Seven to eight.

Group size
Groups of six.

What you need
Soft balls.

What to do
Divide the children into teams of six and tell one child in each team to float on her back. The other children in her team

should swim round the floating child in a circle. At a signal from you, the swimmers must scatter to touch the side of the pool while the floating child has to swim after them and try to tag one child before he touches the side. If a child is caught, he replaces the floater in the centre of the circle. If no one is tagged then the original floater takes up her position again.

Progress to playing body tag where the swimmers in each team do not have the sanctuary of the pool side. Instead they must swim anywhere to avoid the chasing swimmer. To start each game, call out a part of the body which the chasing child must tag.

When the children become even more adept you could be more specific about the parts of the body you nominate; for example 'left foot', 'right hand' and so on.

Finish the session with a general game of ball tag. One child should start the game by throwing a large soft ball at the other children who are swimming about the pool. These children must try to dodge the ball and anyone struck should take over as the thrower.

5. Water ball games

Age range
Seven to eight.

Group size
Individuals and small groups.

What you need
Variety of balls.

What to do
Start this session with a warm-up, where you float a rubber ring in the water and the children have to swim to within 5m of the ring and try to throw a ball into its centre. They will have to tread water as they aim. Repeat the game, increasing the distance of the throw from 5m to 10m and then 12m.

From this warm-up the children can play a team game. Place one team opposite another with a rubber ball half way between the two. At the command, the first child in each team should swim for the ball. The first to reach the ball must then throw it at the side of the pool, scoring one point if it hits the poolside. The second child in each team must then swim for the ball and so on.

End the session with a modified game of water-polo in which the children play in teams of five. As soon as a child receives the ball she must stop swimming, tread water and pass to another child. No child may take a ball from another. The object is to pass the ball swiftly in the water from one player to another until one child can throw the ball against the side of the pool to score a goal.

6. Teaching the arm action for the breast-stroke

Age range
Seven to eight.

Group size
Individuals and pairs.

What you need
Floats.

What to do
Allow the children to swim freely using the front crawl or the backstroke. Congratulate them on the progress they have made and tell them that they are now ready to learn another swimming stroke. Teach and demonstrate the arm action for the breast-stroke. Tell the children to stand in shallow water and practise the action. They should stretch their arms out in front of them with their hands together and their palms outwards and their fingers together. Tell them to move their arms outwards and downwards in a circling movement, ending with their arms out to their sides, level with the shoulders. They should return their hands to a position in front of their faces with their elbows tucked in against their chests and push their arms forward and repeat the stroke.

Having practised the stroke out of the water, ask the children to work in pairs, with one child supporting the others face. The supported child should practise the breast-stroke arm action in the water while lying on her stomach. Make sure the children change places after a while.

To add variety, give the children a chance to practise the arm action while tucking their feet under the rail at the side of the pool. Once they can do this they can crouch with their feet on the bottom of the pool, practising the arm action for the breast-stroke.

Finally, encourage the children to use the arm action while resting their legs on a float.

7. Teaching the leg action for the breast-stroke

Age range
Seven to eight.

Group size
Individuals and pairs.

What you need
Floats.

What to do
Let the children practise the breast-stroke arm action individually and in pairs. You can then teach them the accompanying leg action.

Tell the children to hold on to the rail and let their legs

trail out behind them. Ask them to draw their heels up to their bottoms, keeping their knees together and their heels slightly apart. Tell them to turn their toes out and push back with their feet, until their legs are fully extended.

Let the children practise this at the rail for some time and then put them in pairs, one supporting the other. Make sure the children change positions regularly, as one child holds the other and the second child practises the leg action of the breast-stroke.

Finally, allow the children to move about the pool while holding a float and with their hands uisng the breast stroke action.

Further activity
Let the children take several sessions to allow the children to put the arm and leg actions of the breast-stroke together.

8. Sculling

Age range
Eight to nine.

Group size
Individuals.

What you need
Floats.

What to do
Tell the children that the sculling action will enable them to rest in the water if they become tired while swimming. They should have already done a basic sculling action and so take the opportunity to revise and refine it. Tell the children to float on their backs with their hands cupped close to their sides. They should then smoothly draw their palms through the water in a continuous inward and outward motion.

Allow the children to practise this basic sculling

action and then ask them to experiment with the movements of their hands so that they move in a particular direction. It may be necessary to help a number of the children, but some should be able to discover for themselves that by exerting pressure in a downward direction they will remain stationary in the water. To move backwards the pressure should be directed towards their feet, while to move forward the cupped hands should be drawn back towards their heads.

When most children have mastered these techniques see if they can obey instructions to change direction; for example, 'stay still', 'forward' and 'backward'.

Ask the children to continue with the sculling motion, but this time alter the shape and position of their bodies. What will happen if they draw their knees up to their chins? Can they still scull if they move over on to their sides and then on to their stomachs? Can any of them move into a vertical position in the water and continue sculling? Can they change direction while adopting this posture?

If any children experience difficulty with sculling on their backs, allow them to practise the movement while holding a small float between their thighs.

9. Rotating

Age range
Eight to nine.

Group size
Individuals and small groups.

What you need
No special requirements.

What to do
Tell the children that it may sometimes be important to be able to change position in the water from their fronts to their backs and from their backs on to their fronts. Tell the children to float on their stomachs and make a right-

hand turn on to their backs by turning their heads to the right, while at the same time dropping their right shoulders. At the same time they should scull with their hands to accomplish the turn on to their back.

In order to turn back on to their stomachs in the same direction, they should incline their heads and turn to the right again, adjusting the sculling motion until the turn is accomplished.

Let the children repeat the exercise, this time making a left turn from their stomachs to their backs by dropping their left shoulders and inclining their heads while sculling until they are floating on their backs. They should then drop their left shoulders to rotate back on to their stomachs. Allow the children to practise alternately making left and right rotations.

End the session by organising a relay race between teams from one side

of the pool to the other. Each child in turn should scull across the width of the pool, making one right-hand rotation and one left-hand rotation, and then turn and scull back, making another right-hand and left-hand rotation, before handing over to the next child in the team and so on.

10. Treading water

Age range
Eight to nine.

Group size
Individuals.

What you need
No special requirements.

What to do
Tell the children to adopt a vertical position in the water and scull gently with their

hands to keep still. Ask them to experiment with a number of leg positions. Explain to them that treading water is often used in life-saving situations, so it will be necessary for them to try to save energy. What is the least energetic leg movement they can find which will allow them to remain vertical in the water, assisted only by gentle sculling movements of the hands?

Ask the more successful children to demonstrate the leg movements they have adopted for this purpose. Some will probably have worked out a gentle cycling motion while others may have chosen to swing their legs gently from the hips. See how many different leg motions have been devised in the class and encourage the children to experiment with all of them in turn.

End the session by timing to see how long the children can tread water without discomfort.

11. Surface dive

Age range
Eight to nine.

Group size
Individuals.

What you need
No special requirements

What to do
Ask the children to practise the surface dive. They should float on their stomachs in the water. Tell them to sweep their arms to the side and back in a powerful thrust. At the same time tell them to bend forwards from the waist and push their heads and shoulders down into the water. They must then scoop their arms back through the water until they are pointing down, in line with their bodies. This

should bring their legs up into a vertical position and send the children diving down to the bottom of the pool.

Give the children plenty of time to practise this movement. Tell them to experiment with different arm movements as they begin their vertical dive to the bottom of the pool.

12. Feet first dive

Age range
Eight to nine.

Group size
Individuals.

What you need
No special requirements.

What to do
Teach and demonstrate the feet first dive. Tell the children to begin by treading water. They should then spread their arms out in the water and push downwards with their arms and legs, forcing their bodies upwards. They should place their arms at their sides and adopt a position of standing to

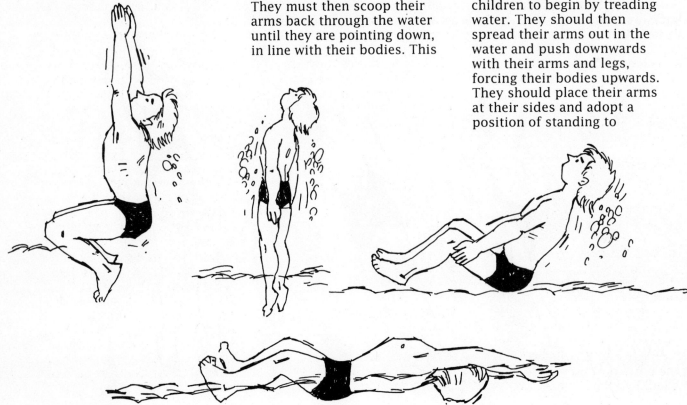

attention. Their bodies will then re-enter the water and sink to the bottom.

Allow the children to practise this dive and encourage them to experiment with different arm movements as they go down. They could also try thrusting with their feet and legs when they reach the bottom of the pool to prepare to return to the surface.

13. Handstands

Age range
Eight to nine.

Group size
Individuals.

What you need
No special requirements.

What to do
Tell the children to stand in the water so that it reaches up to their shoulders. They should then raise their hands as far as they can above their heads and plunge forward into a dive. When their hands reach the bottom of the pool they should adjust them so that

they are shoulder-width apart. Finally, they should straighten their hands and arms and try to maintain a handstand position.

Allow the children to practise this, but do not force any of the more nervous ones to do more than they want to. Encourage the more adept ones to practise walking a few steps on their hands while under water. The children could also work in pairs and devise underwater positions and patterns involving handstands.

14. Fall dive

Age range
Eight to nine.

Group size
Individuals.

What you need
Floats.

What to do
The fall dive is the easiest method of diving from the

side of a pool. However, it is vital that you check that the depth of the water is adequate before the children attempt to dive.

Ask the children to stand on the edge of the pool, gripping the ledge with their toes. They should extend their arms and lower their heads between them. Tell them to fix their eyes on the area of water where they are likely to enter. They should then bend their knees and crouch forward, bringing their bottoms up high and making sure that their hands are touching. Tell them to hold the balance for a few seconds and then topple forward into the water, pushing away from the ledge by straightening their legs. They should keep their heads tucked between their outstretched arms and break the surface of the water with their hands and arms, gliding forward through the water and then up to the surface.

Under strict supervision, allow the children to practise this dive. Two or three sessions will probably be necessary before all the children have enough confidence to allow themselves to overbalance from the side of the pool into the water.

To encourage the children and give them confidence organise a number of competitions. Allow each child to do three dives and use floats secured to the bottom of the pool to see where each one breaks the surface after the dive. See which child makes the longest dive. Also organise other dives where the children have to kick with their legs just once when they reach the surface. Who can glide the furthest across the pool?

Further activity

When the children have mastered the fall dive they may progress to the upright fall dive. This time they should stand on the side of the pool in an upright position, not a crouched one. They should raise their arms out to their sides until they extend between the head and shoulders. The dive is started by the children bending their knees slightly and then falling forwards. At the same time, they should bring their arms forward together so that their palms are touching. Remind them to straighten their legs before their arms and bodies enter the water.

15. Front crawl turn

Age range
Nine to ten.

Group size
Individuals and small groups.

What you need
No special requirements.

What to do

Once the children can swim more than a width, they should be shown how to turn when they reach the side of the pool. To do this the child should approach the side of the pool using the front crawl and touch the end of the pool with his leading hand. As he touches the side he should bend his arm slightly and turn his body onto his side, bringing up his knees to his chest and lifting up his head. He should then swing his legs round and place the soles of his feet against the side of the pool and push off with his feet. At the same time he should adopt a streamlined body shape and glide through the water before starting the front crawl once more.

Give the children ample time to practise this movement and then organise a series of two-width relay races in which each child swims a width using the front crawl, performs the front crawl turn and then swims back to touch the next child in the team and so on.

16. Breast-stroke turn

Age range
Nine to ten.

Group size
Individuals and small groups.

What you need
No special requirements.

What to do
Teach and demonstrate the breast-stroke turn. To do this the child should approach the side of the pool using the breast-stroke, grasp the rail and raise her head. She should then let go with one hand and allow her legs to drop, turning to one side in the process. She should then swing round, releasing her grip with the remaining hand, and placing both feet firmly against the side of the pool, pushing off vigorously into a glide from which she resumes the breast-stroke.

Give the children plenty of time to practise this turn and then organise relay races in which the children cover two widths of the pool, using the breast-stroke turn.

17. Backstroke turn

Age range
Nine to ten.

Group size
Individuals and small groups.

What you need
No special requirements.

What to do
Teach the backstroke turn. To do this the child should approach the side of the pool using the backstroke and glance over his shoulder so that he can reach out and touch the side with his leading hand. He should then rotate on to his front and tuck his knees up and place his second hand on the side of the pool as well. Putting both feet against the side, he should release his grip and kick off, extending both his hands behind his head into a streamlined glide before resuming the backstroke movement.

Allow the children to practise this turn and then put it into action in a series of two-width backstroke races involving using the backstroke turn at the end of the first width.

18. Integrated swimming activities: 1

Age range
Nine to ten.

Group size
Small groups and the whole class.

What you need
Floats, buoyancy aids.

What to do
In the classroom before the swimming session tell the children the story of Aesop's 'The viper, the frogs and the water snake' (*Fables from Aesop*, retold by James Reeves, Blackie). In this story the viper and the water snake fight for supremacy in a pond. The frogs living in the pond wish to support the viper, but all they can think to do is croak loudly. The viper overcomes the water snake and the delighted frogs ask for a share of the spoils. The viper merely whistles. He tells the bewildered frogs that he is repaying them in the way they helped him – by making a useless noise.

Tell the children that you are going to put them in teams and you want them to act out Aesop's story in the water, making a form of water ballet. In each team one child should be the viper, one the water snake and the remainder will be the frogs.

Give the children plenty of time to discuss and plan their ballets. How will an onlooker

be able to tell who is who in the story? Obviously the viper and the water snake will have to swim differently and the frogs will have to select a third stroke. What sort of stroke do they think most closely resembles a frog in the water? What does a snake look like when it glides along? Will any aids be needed to represent the rushes and rocks?

When the swimming session starts, let each team practise together for some time and then let them demonstrate what they have put together. How are they going to enter and leave the water? How can the fight be staged with neither child getting hurt? What will the water snake look like after it has been slain?

When all the teams have had their chance to perform their ballets, choose the best viper and the most realistic water snake and ask all the other children in the class to be the frogs and stage the story once more.

Further activity

Other stories which could be used as the basis for similar water ballets are:
• *The Frog Prince* by the Brothers Grimm (Walker Books, 1991).
• *The Water Babies* by Charles Kingsley (Gollancz, 1986).
• 'The Incredible Jumping Frog' by Mark Twain in *A Collection of Animal Stories* ed. G. Kent (Brimax).

19. Integrated swimming activities: 2

Age range
Nine to ten.

Group size
Small groups and the whole class.

What you need
Floats, other buoyancy aids.

What to do
In the classroom, tell the children the story of 'The Ugly Duckling'. In this story a strange egg rolls into a clutch being hatched by a duck. One by one the ducklings emerge from the eggs and slip easily into the water. The final egg

hatches and a strange, ugly creature emerges and flaps clumsily into the pond. The other ducklings swim well and easily, but the latest arrival is clumsy and laughed at by the others. Eventually they grow and it is apparent that the ugly duckling is really a beautiful swan. The swan swims away and then flies back to its own kind.

Ask the children to split up into teams and arrange how they are going to mime the story of in the water, using as many props as they wish.

When the swimming session starts, encourage the children who are playing the parts of ducklings to swim as well as they can, performing as many swimming and floating tricks as they know, while the ugly duckling flounders and makes mistakes.

Let each team practise together and then demonstrate their water ballet. What happens when each emerges from the shell? How does their mother look after them in the water? What will the ugly duckling do?

When all the teams have had a chance to perform their ballets, select the best ugly duckling and most impressive mother duck, and ask all the other children to be ducklings in a class performance of the story.

Further activity
Other stories which could be used as the basis for further water ballets could be:
• *Jonah and the Lord* by George Macbeth (Macmillan).
• *Tarka the Otter* by Henry Williamson (Puffin, 1971).
• *Dr Doolittle and the Secret Lake* by Hugh Lofting (Cape).
• 'The Lord Fish' by Walter de la Mare in *Animal Stories* (Faber).

Survival skills

1. The basic grips

Age range
Ten to eleven.

Group size
Pairs.

What you need
No special requirements.

What to do
Ask the children to stand in pairs in shallow water. Designate one child in each pair to be the life-saver and the other to be the person being saved. Ask the saver to stand behind the subject and demonstrate the basic life-saving grip. To do this, the saver should place one arm over the subject's shoulder and grasp her chin between her thumb and first finger. Tell the savers to imagine that they are holding guns, with the thumb on the safety catch and the first finger on the trigger.

Allow both children in each pair to demonstrate and practise this grip, taking it in turns to stand in front. When the children seem to have grasped it, allow them to practise the grip in the water. To do this the subject should float on her back while the saver kneels in the water

behind her. The saver then places his arm over her shoulder and adopts the 'gun' grip. It may be necessary at this early stage for the saver to support the subject by placing his hand and arm under the back of the floating child, using his other hand.

Allow the children to practise this grip in the water, changing places frequently.

Further activity
Allow the children to practise a variation of the gun grip which is usually used on swimmers who have lost consciousness. To do this the children adopt the same position, behind the subject with thumb and first finger holding the jaw, but then the saver draws the subject closer to him. If the saver is using his right hand and arm, then his left cheek should be next to and touching the right cheek of the subject, giving complete control. Let the children practise this grip in pairs, first standing in the water and then kneeling in the water with the subject floating on her back.

If there is time, teach the chest grip, whereby the saver places one arm across the chest of the subject, gripping the child with his hand some way below her arm-pit.

2. Combining basic grips with swimming strokes

Age range
Ten to eleven.

Group size
Pairs.

What you need
No special requirements.

What to do
Tell the children that you want them to practise the three basic grips they learned in the last activity. As before, they should practise this first with one child standing behind the other and then with one child floating on her back while the other kneels behind her in the water.

Tell the children that they are going to learn how to do the leg and arm strokes which go with these survival grips.

This will enable them to bring someone to the side of the pool. If the right hand is being used for the gun grip, the first child should hold the second child by the chin with his first finger and thumb from his right hand, the right arm being placed over the right shoulder of the second child. The first child should then go over on to his right side, so that his right arm is submerged, but still retaining the grip on the chin of the second child. Still on his side, the child should use a scissors kick – kicking alternately with either leg while on his side. His free left arm will be on top and should be used to make sculling movements to take the second child to the side of the pool.

Allow the children to practise this in their own depth, helping and encouraging them as they work. The same arm and leg movements may be used for all three grips.

The class will probably need at least two or three sessions and perhaps more before they can be expected to master the combinations of movements

required. However, when they have grasped the technique tell them that when they swim out to help a child in difficulties they should try to use a stroke which enables them to keep their heads above water, so that they can call out encouragement and any instructions.

3. Rope throwing

Age range
Ten to eleven.

Group size
Pairs.

What you need
Lightweight ropes about 20m long.

What to do
Tell the children that it is very important that any ropes used for life-saving purposes are coiled neatly before and after use. Demonstrate how to throw one end of a rope, using an under-arm throw, as far as possible into the water, while retaining the other end.

You should then put the children in pairs and give each pair a rope. One child in each pair should stand some way

out in the water while the other child stands on the side of the pool. Tell the child on the side to retain one end of the rope and throw the other end to the child in the pool, using the under-arm throw. Let them practise this until the rope begins to land near the child who is in the water.

Each time that the rope is reeled in, check that it is brought to the side properly without getting tangled. To do this the child should stand sideways on to the pool and place her right hand firmly against her right knee with her palm facing outwards. The rope should be reeled in with her left hand and then fed to the stationary right hand, forming a series of coils of the same length. When the entire length has been reeled in the child may drop the coils at her feet.

Having done this the children can progress to throwing the rope and then reeling it in with the child in the water clinging on to it with both hands. To do this the child standing on the side should face the pool and drag the other child to the side using a hand-over-hand pull. When the child in the water reaches the side of the pool he should place both his hands on top of the pool and climb

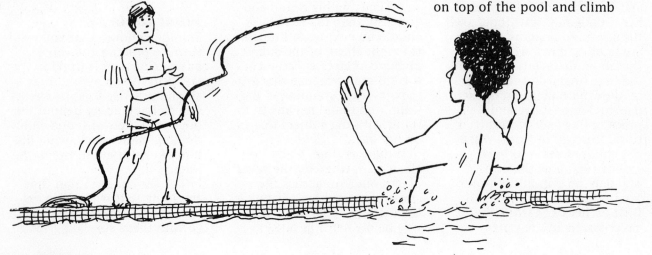

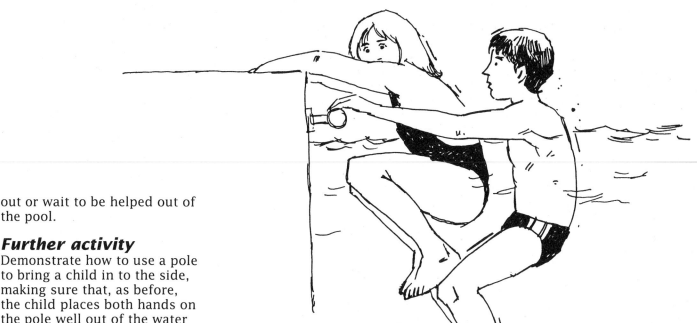

out or wait to be helped out of the pool.

Further activity

Demonstrate how to use a pole to bring a child in to the side, making sure that, as before, the child places both hands on the pole well out of the water as he is dragged to safety.

4. Helping a child out of the water

Age range
Ten to eleven.

Group size
Pairs and groups of three.

What you need
Rope, pole.

What to do

Practise the various methods of fetching a child in difficulties to the side of the pool – using the rope, pole and fetching the child to the side in one of the grips already learned. Then let the children practise getting a child out of the pool once she has reached the side. The children should work in pairs and assume that one of them has just been brought to the side of the pool and is hanging on with extended hands well over the side of the pool.

The other child in each pair should jump into the water

and come up behind the child who is clinging to the side. This second child should hold on to the rail and place his left hand under the left arm-pit of the child, and his right hand under the right arm-pit of the child.

The rescued child should bring up her knees, so that she is in a crouching position, with her knees against the side of the pool. The other child should then slide his knees under her feet so that they act as a step for the child in front. He should then bring his face close to the ear of the child in front, in order to communicate with her and, if necessary to calm and reassure her. He should order the child in front to put her feet on his knees and thus lift herself out of the water and on to the side of the pool.

Still speaking with calm authority, the saver should then order the child who has climbed out of the water to move away from the pool and sit with her back to the water. This is to help the rescued child recover from any sense of shock and at the same time

permit the rescuer to go back across the pool if someone else needs rescuing.

Further activity

If the children seem to be fairly competent when rescuing one child, organise them into threes and ask one child to bring two children out of the water. The second child should cling to the side of the pool and the third child should swim farther out in the pool. The first child will need to jump into the water and help 0the second child out by providing a step with his knees. It is important that he then makes sure that the second child walks away from the pool for a few metres and sits with her back to the pool. Only then should the first child swim out to the middle of the pool and bring in the third child, using one of the holds already practised.

5. Using floats

Age range
Ten to eleven.

Group size
Pairs.

What you need
Floats, balls, empty plastic containers, quoits.

What to do
Organise the children into pairs and tell them that you want one child in each pair to help the other to reach the side of the pool by using a variety of objects which will float and which will enable the child to remain above water until she is saved.

Ask the children who are to be rescued to swim about the pool so that they are some distance from each other. The other children should stand on the side and find a number of different objects which will float and throw them, one at a time, to their partners, and ask them to cling to them.

The rescuers should then enter the water and swim towards the children to be rescued second child. They should shout 'I am coming to you!' and tell the children in the water to grasp the floating object and kick out towards them. When the rescuers meet their partners they should hold on to the floating objects or the arms of the children being rescued and guide them to the side of the pool.

Ask the children to experiment with different floating objects, methods of holding on to them and types of swimming strokes.

Further activity
In order to emphasise that many different objects may be used to help a swimmer in trouble, ask pairs of children to experiment with a rubber quoit. The child in the water should clasp one side of the quoit while the rescuer holds the other side of the quoit and tows the child to the side of the pool.

6. Team activity

Age range
Ten to eleven.

Group size
Small groups.

What you need
Arm bands, rope, pole.

What to do
Organise the children into teams of six or seven. As with all survival techniques make sure that all the children involved can swim well. The intention is to *give* children confidence, so that when they find other children in difficulties in the water they will know what to do.

Ask one team of children to get into the water and scatter. Do not let the other children see where the children in the water have been placed. At a signal, the members of the second team should go to the side of the pool and see where the children in the first team are situated. They must then lower themselves into the water – they must not jump or dive in, in case one of the children to be rescued is floating unobserved close to the side of the pool. Each child in the second team must then swim to a child in the first team and bring him back to the side of the pool and help him out of the water. When the children have had plenty of practice, the teams can be timed to see which gets another team out of the water in the fastest time.

A variation on this is to give some of the children in the water an arm band to wear. This indicates that the child is 'unconscious' and therefore the rescuer should adopt the close or cheek-to-cheek rescue grip. The other children may choose whether to use the ordinary gun grip, the chest grip, throwing a rope or throwing floating objects and swimming after them.

CHAPTER 7

Planning and assessment

The amount of time to be allocated to each of the components of the PE curriculum is a knotty problem. As practitioners ourselves, we are only too well aware of the complexities of trying to compile a class timetable. However, it is generally held by the specialists in the field that the PE provision can best be covered if a total of some two hours a week is devoted to it, perhaps, but not necessarily, divided into four 30-minute periods.

If we sense a general reaction of derision, accompanied by snorts of 'chance would be a fine thing', we can only resort to the uneasy panacea we have been offering to the children we teach for more years than we care to remember, 'Do the best you can!'

In the suggestions given in this chapter we advocate devoting each term to one or two strands of the physical education programme. This does not mean, of course, that the other areas need be ignored. If the main topics to be covered in a particular term are games and outdoor activities, for example, then periods may still be devoted to gymnastics and dance.

If you decide to work so that you allocate two strands to each term, the following is an example of how such as programme could be organised. Also a programme planning sheet is provided on photocopiable page 192.

Reception class (age four to five)

Autumn term
• Gymnastics: locomotion and partner work.
• Dance: bonfire night.

Spring term
• Gymnastics: locomotion and partner work.
• Games: throwing and catching, small team games.

Summer term
• Dance: fairy tales.
• Games: running, travelling with a ball, simple relay games.

Year 1 (five to six)

Autumn term
• Gymnastics: balance.

• Dance: fairground.

Spring term
• Games: basic ball skills.
• Dance: a windy day.

Summer term
• Gymnastics: balance.
• Games: running, travelling with a ball, simple relay games.

Year 2 (age six to seven)

Autumn term
• Gymnastics: twist and turn.
• Dance: playground games.

Spring term
• Games: using bats and balls.
• Dance: sports based theme e.g. swimming.

Summer term
Gymnastics: twist and turn.
Dance: running, travelling with a ball, simple relay games.

Year 3 (age seven to eight)

Autumn term
• Gymnastics: tip, twist, swing roll.
• Dance: clowns, skating, wheels and so on.

Spring term
• Outdoor activities: including exploring the environment, simple orienteering.

Summer term
• Athletics: walking, sprinting, throwing.
• Swimming: water familiarisation, floating, basic strokes.

Year 4 (age eight to nine)

Autumn term
• Gymnastics: contracting and stretching.
• Dance: robots, the rodeo, shipwrecks and so on.

Spring term
Outdoor activities: including cycling and expeditions.

Summer term
• Athletics: walking, sprinting, throwing, jumping.
• Swimming: basic strokes, relays, standing dives while in the water.

Year 5 (age nine to ten)

Autumn term
• Gymnastics: flight.
• Dance: the jungle, the supermarket, the orchestra and so on.

Spring term
• Games: hockey, football, netball.
• Outdoor activities: including camping.

Summer term
• Athletics: longer distances for running, throwing, jumping.
• Swimming: attaining a 25m distance.

Year 6 (age ten to eleven)

Autumn term
• Gymnastics: partner work. Dance: the circus, traffic police, Noah's ark and so on.

Spring term
• Games: hockey, football, netball.
• Outdoor activities: including orienteering.

Summer term
• Athletics: running, throwing, jumping.
• Games: rounders, cricket.

Assessment

There are four purposes to assessment:
• formative – are the children coping with each task? Is it too easy?
• diagnostic – what can be done to help those children who are not achieving or who are especially gifted?
• summative – a summary of a term, half-year or year's work.
• evaluative – evaluates the work of a school, for example, ensuring standardisation and improvement of standards.

Assessment is used to:
• inform parents and other teachers;
• show progress;
• ensure that the work being undertaken is appropriate for the child.

The National Curriculum has only one attainment target for physical education, so this means that the end of key stage statements will be used for assessment should be continuous and not a 'bolt on' process. When looking to see whether individuals have achieved the requirements of each key stage for each part of the physical education curriculum you should look to assess them at or as near to the end of each key stage as possible. Assessment procedures should be simple and based on your own judgement of the children's performances.

Strands of the curriculum
The following shows each part of the PE curriculum together with the National Curriculum requirements for each key stage.

Athletics
• Key Stage 2: run with speed; jump with height and distance; throw with accuracy; measure; improve.

Dance

Key Stage 1: dance with speed, tension and continuity; dance using different shapes, directions and levels; to dance to different stimuli; explore moods and feelings; develop rhythmic responses; include traditional dance.

• Key Stage 2: make dances involving beginnings, middles and ends, step patterns and different body parts; create simple characters and narratives in movement describe and interpret different elements of dance. Traditional British Isles dances should also be included, as should dance from different times and places.

Games

• Key Stage 1: use a variety of equipment; practise receiving and travelling with a ball; experience games involving dodging, avoiding, awareness of space and others; make up simple games with rules and objectives.

• Key Stage 2: understand common skills of invasion, net/wall and striking/fielding games; develop own games; play simplified versions of recognised games.

Gymnastics

• Key Stage 1: experience and refine basic actions of travelling, turning, rolling, jumping, balancing, swinging, climbing and taking weight on hands; practise and refine individual actions; link a series of actions together; carry and position simple apparatus.

• Key Stage 2: use the floor and apparatus for rolling, jumping, swinging, balancing and taking weight on hands; be guided to perform in a controlled manner and understand that the ending of one action can become the beginning of the next; explore and refine longer series of actions on the floor and apparatus; respond to a variety of tasks emphasising changing speed, shape and direction through gymnastic actions.

Outdoor and adventurous activities

• Key Stage 2: explore potential for physical activities within the immediate environment; undertake simple orientation activities;

apply physical skills out of doors on suitable equipment; develop awareness of basic safety practices.

Understand principles of safety while responding to a variety of challenges; experience outdoor and adventurous activities in different environments that involve planning, navigation, working in groups and recording and evaluating; to be taught appropriate skills.

Swimming

Whether swimming is taught in Key Stage 1 or 2 depends on the teacher. However, the following requirements will need to be met; learn codes of pool hygiene and courtesy; develop confidence by learning to rest and float in water; learn different methods of propulsion in water; develop swimming strokes on the front and back; learn principles of water safety; learn appropriate survival skills; assess own skills; play simple water games; swim a distance of 25m.

AT CHARTS

England and Wales

There is only one attainment target in the National Curriculum for Physical Education for England and Wales which consists of the sum total of the knowledge, skills and understanding involved in the process of planning, performing and evaluating which children are expected to demonstrate by the end of each Key Stage.

This attainment target emphasises the process of *planning*, *performing* and *evaluating* in each aspect of the curriculum covered by the children. These can be seen as strands running through the Programmes of Study, but they cannot be taught separately as the process is holistic, and therefore the activities in this book reflect this integration.

The model of progression shown below illustrates the process of plan, perform and evaluate which the children are to be taught and which can be applied to all the activities. This will take the form of a slow build-up in which the children at Key Stage 1 will be working with the emphasis on **perform**, but at the same time will be working towards being able to **plan** and **evaluate** their performance.

You should direct the children's attention to the process by asking questions during the lesson, for example, 'Can you find another way of doing...', 'Can you show me...?' etc. Encourage the best possible work from the children so that they are always striving for improvement. In time this should lead to the children becoming more independent, asking themselves if they can improve their work and so seeking quality in their performance. Endeavour also to help the children become more interactive, both competitively and co-operatively. This may be achieved in small team games, or by working with a partner in, say, gymnastics.

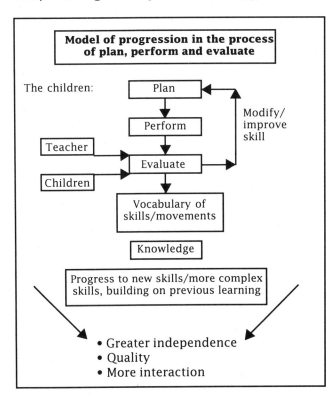

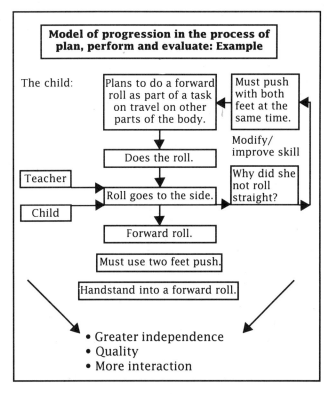

Scotland

The chart on this page refers to the Scottish curriculum for Physical Education. Activities are identified by their chapter and activity number: for example, **2**/1 means Chapter 2, Activity 1. Where activities are organised in themes within chapters, these are indicated by the use of initial letters as shown in the key. Thus **3**/SGS is Chapter 3, 'Simple games skills'.

Key
Chapter 3: SGS = Simple games skills, ST = Short tennis, R = Rounders, F = Football, N = Netball, H= Hockey, C = Cricket
Chapter 4: L = Locomotion, B = Balance, TT = Twist and turn, B2 = Balance 2, CS = Contract and Stretch, F = Flight, DFPW = Different form of partner work
Chapter 6: IW = Introduction to the water, FM = Floating and moving, SWA = Swimming without aids, SS = Survival skills

Strands \ Levels	A	B	C	D	E
Investigating and developing fitness	1/1-3; 6/IW	1/1-4; 6/FM	6/FM, SWA	1/8; 6/SWA, SS	1/8; 6/SWA, SS
Using the body	1/1-3; **2**/1; 3/SGS; 4/L, B; 5/1-3, 5-8; 6/IW	1/1-5; **2**/1-2; 3/SGS; 4/L, B, TT; 5/17, 19, 22; 6/IW, FM	1/5-6; **2**/3, 5-6; 3/ST, R, F, N; 4/TT, B2, CS; 5/17, 19, 22; 6/FM, SWA	1/5-7; **2**/6, 9; 3/F, N, H; 4/B2, CS, F, DFPW; 6/SWA, SS	**2**/6, 9; 3/H, C; 4/F, DFPW; 6/SWA, SS
Applying skills	1/3; **2**/1; 3/SGS; 4/L, B; 5/1-3, 5-8; 13-15; 6/IW	1/3-4; **2**/1-2; 3/SGS; 4/L, B, TT; 5/5-6, 13-15, 17-19, 22-25; 6/IW, FM	**2**/3-6; 3/ST, R, F, N; 4/TT, B2, CS; 5/17-19, 22-25, 27-28, 30-32; 6/FM, SWA	1/8; **2**/4-9; 3/F, N, H; 4/B2, CS, F, DFPW; 5/27-28, 30-38; 6/SWA, SS	1/8; **2**/6, 9; 3/C; 4/F, DFPW; 5/33-38; 6/SWA, SS
Creating and designing	**2**/1; 4/L, B; 5/1-7, 9-12, 14-16	**2**/1-2; 4/L, B, TT; 5/9-12, 14-16, 18-23, 25; 6/FM	**2**/3-6; 4/TT, B2; 5/18-23, 25, 30-32; 6/FM, SWA	**2**/5-9; 4/B2, CS, F, DFPW; 5/30-38; 6/SWA, SS	**2**/7-9; 4/F, DFPW; 5/33-38; 6/SWA, SS
Co-operating, sharing, communicating and competing	1/1-2; **2**/1; 3/SGS; 4/L, B; 5/1-8; 10-11, 14-16; 6/IW	1/1-2; **2**/1-2; 3/SGS; 4/L, B, TT; 5/10-11, 14-16, 18-22, 24-25; 6/IW, FM	**2**/3-6; 3/ST, R, F, N; 4/TT, B2; 5/18-22, 24-25, 27-28, 30-31; 6/FM, SWA	**2**/7-9; 3/F, N, H; 4/B2, CS, DFPW; 5/27-28, 30-31, 33-38; 6/SWA, SS	**2**/7-9; 3/C; 4/DFPW; 5/33-38; 6/SWA, SS
Observing, reflecting, describing and responding	1/1; 4/L, B; 5/7, 10-12, 14	**2**/3; 4/L, B, TT; 5/10-12, 14, 17, 20, 22-23, 25	**2**/3, 7-9; 4/TT, B2; 5/17, 20, 22-23, 25, 27-28; 6/SWA	**2**/7-9; 4/B2, CS, DFPW; 5/27-28, 33, 38; 6/SWA, SS	**2**/7-9; 4/DFPW; 5/33, 38; 6/SWA, SS

CHAPTER 8

Resources

Detailed rules of different games and advice on technique are often provided in official handbooks published by the governing bodies of organisations or in books written with the approval of these bodies.

An excellent series is 'Know the Game' published by A&C Black. Among the sports covered in this series are athletics, camping, cricket, gymnastics, life saving and water safety, map reading, orienteering, rounders, short tennis, soccer, swimming and volleyball.

Other books which have been written in collaboration with various sporting bodies include:

• *The MCC Cricket Coaching Book* (MCC/Heinemann/Kingswood).

• *Guide to the Introduction of Short Tennis* (Lawn Tennis Association).

• *Curriculum Volleyball Level 1 Coaching Manual* (English Volleyball Association).

• *Swimming, teaching and coaching Level 1* and *Swimming for those with Special Needs* (Amateur Swimming Association).

• *Safety in Outdoor Education* (DES/HMSO).

Two comprehensive collections of rules and equipment of sports and games are:

• *Rules and Equipment of the Game*, compiled by Ivan Morrison (Pelham Books, out of print).

• *Rules of the Game: Complete illustrated encyclopaedia of all the sports of the world* (Collins Willow).

The following list of books has been divided according to subject area. Not all the books are geared to specific National Curriculum requirements, but each provides a wealth of sensible and practical activities which can be adapted for specific needs.

General
• Roberts, Catherine, *Go for it!: PE activities for the classroom teacher* (Oxford University Press). This book provides sequential lessons in the main areas of physical education.

• Severs, John, *Activities for PE using Small Apparatus* (Simon and Schuster). This book provides activities for children from Reception to Year 8, using bean bags, balls, ropes, hoops and so on.

Safety
• British Association of Advisers and Lecturers in Physical Education, *Safe Practice in Physical Education* (White Line Press). This is an encyclopaedic collection of tips on safety precautions for children engaged in PE.

Dance
• Oliver, Susan, *Creative movement, Dance Ideas for Primary Teachers* (Mary Glasgow). This is a collection of 18 sample lessons covering Key Stages 1 and 2 and ranging over a wide variety of themes. The book includes a cassette of specially-written music to accompany the dance suggestions.

Gymnastics
• Trevor, M.D., *The Development of Gymnastic Skills: A scheme of work for teachers* (Simon and Schuster). This book contains 200 gymnastics activities for primary school children.

- Underwood, Martin, *Agile* (Nelson). This consists of 96 double-sided gymnastic work-cards for children aged between eight and fourteen. It is accompanied by a video and a teacher's guide and record book.

Health
- Sykes, K. and Beaumont, G., *Exercise and Health* (Longman). This book is concerned with health-focused PE for schools.

Problems
- Stewart, David, *The Right to Movement* (Falmer Press). This book looks at ways for teachers to help 'clumsy' children in PE lessons.

General games
- Cooper, Andrew, *The Development of Games Skills: A scheme of work for teachers* (Simon and Schuster). This book suggests games activities for Years 4 to 7.

- Heseltine, Peter, *Games for All Children* (Simon and Schuster). This book provides games which stress co-operation rather than competition for children, from reception to Year 6.

Athletics
- Couling, David, *Athletics: a handbook for teachers* (Hale, out of print). This provides basic techniques for running, jumping and throwing.

- Dick, Frank, *But first* (British Athletics Federation). This is recommended as a beginners coaching manual by the Amateur Athletics Association.

Cricket
- Benaud, L.R., *The Young Cricketer* (Angus and Robertson). This provides basic bowling, batting and fielding techniques.

- Boycott, G., *Geoff Boycott's Book for Young Cricketers* (Stanley Paul). More basic coaching tips!

Soccer
- Hughes, Charles, *The FA Coaching Book of Soccer Tactics* (BBC/Leonard/Queen Anne Press). Excellent advice from beginners to advanced players.

Basketball
- Bunnett, Chris and McSweeney, Sean, *Know about Basketball* (AA Publishing). This is a succinct, but comprehensive guide to the sport.

Netball
- Martin, Tony, *Netball Fundamentals* (David and Charles, out of print). This provides basic advice for beginners.

- *Netball Rules for Young Players* (All England Netball Association).

Rugby union
Cooke, Geoff, *Skilful Rugby Union* (A & C Black). A top coach sets out his ideas simply, but effectively.

Survival, orienteering, camping

• Watkins, David and Delal, Meike, *Camping and Walking* (Usborne). This is a really first-rate, comprehensive book.

• Poulter, Christine, *Playing the Game* (Macmillan). This book is full of games and activities which are suitable for warm-ups.

Swimming

•Meredith, Susan and Hicks, Carol *Teach your child to swim* and Fischer, Emma *Improving Swimming Skills* (Usbourne). Recommended by the ASA.

• Harrison, Joan *Anyone can swim* (Crowood Press). Helpful for the physically challenged.

Equipment

At the beginning of each school year it is essential that the availability and condition of PE equipment is checked. There is a great deal of excellent equipment on the market, but much of it is expensive. A school should build up its stock of equipment gradually. However, the following equipment must be to hand if the various strands of the PE curriculum is to be covered properly.

Gymnastics

Mats
Benches
Wallbars
Flat-top boxes
Ropes
Climbing frames

Dance

Mats
Cassette player

Athletics

Hoops
Skittles
Markers
Quoits
Small balls
Sacks
Eggs and spoons
Plastic bats
Bean bags
Canes
Size five balls
Tape measures
Stop watches
Cricket balls
Rounders balls
Skipping ropes

Swimming

Floats
Arm bands
Lightweight balls
Pingpong balls
Rubber bricks

Games

Footballs
Netballs
Plastic bats
Bean bags
Quoits
Hoops
Skittles
Sponge balls
Rounders bats
Plastic balls
Mats
Rounders posts
Rounders balls
Netball bibs
Netball posts
Chalk block
Hockey sticks
Hockey balls
Indoor hockey sticks
Pucks
Hockey goalkeeping equipment
Cricket balls
Cricket bats
Wickets
Cricket pads and gloves

Orienteering

Compasses
Clip boards
Plastic folders
Stop-watch

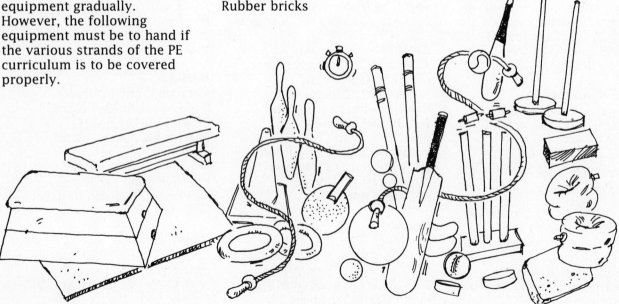

Addresses of sporting bodies

Association Football

Football Association, 16 Lancaster Gate, London W2 3LW.

Scottish Schools Football Association, 5 Forth Park Gardens, Kirkcaldy, Fife KY2 5TD.

Football Association of Wales, Plymouth Chambers, 3 Westgate Street, Cardiff, South Glamorgan.

Athletics

Amateur Athletics Association of England, Edgbaston House, 3 Duchess Place, Hagley Road, Edgbaston, Birmingham B16 8NM.

Scottish Amateur Athletic Association, Caledonia House, South Gyle, Edinburgh EH12 9DQ.

Athletics Association of Wales, Swansea Athletics Stadium, Upper Bank, Landore, Swansea, West Glamorgan SA1 7DF.

Basketball

English Basketball Association, 48 Bradford Road, Stanningley, Leeds LS28 6DF.

Scottish Basketball Association, Caledonia House, South Gyle, Edinburgh EH12 9DQ.

Basketball Association of Wales, 327 Cowbridge Road East, Canton, Cardiff, South Glamorgan CF5 1JD.

Canoeing

British Canoe Union, Adbolton Lane, Westbridgford, Nottinghamshire NG2 5AS.

Scottish Canoe Association, Caledonia House, South Gyle, Edinburgh EH12 9DQ.

Welsh Canoeing Association, Pen-y-Bont, Corwen, Clwyd.

Cricket

National Cricket Association, Lord's Cricket Ground, London NW8 8QZ.

Women's Cricket Association, 41 St Michaels' Lane, Heddingley, Leeds LS6 3BR.

Scottish Cricket Union, Caledonia House, South Gyle, Edinburgh EH12 9DQ.

Welsh Cricket Association, 33 Hendrefoilan Avenue, Sketty, Swansea, West Glamorgan SA2 7NA.

Gymnastics

British Amateur Gymnastics Association, Ford Hall, LNSC, Nr Newport, Shropshire TF10 9NB.

Scottish Amateur Gymnastics Association, 8b Melville Street, Falkirk FK1 1HZ.

Welsh Amateur Gymnastic Association, 39 Wyndham Arcade, Mill Lane, Cardiff, South Glamorgan.

Hockey

Hockey Association, Norfolk House, 102 Saxonsgate West, Milton Keynes MK9 2EP.

Scottish Hockey Union, Caledonia House, South Gyle, Edinburgh EH12 9DQ.

Welsh Hockey Association, 1 White Hart Lane, Caerleon, Gwent NP6 1AB.

Lawn tennis

Lawn Tennis Association Trust, Palliser Road, West Kensington, London W14 9EG.

Scottish Lawn Tennis Association, 12 Melville Crescent, Edinburgh EH3 7LV.

Welsh Lawn Tennis Association, Plymouth Chambers, 3 Westgate Street, Cardiff, South Glamorgan.

Netball
All-England Netball Association, Netball House, 9 Paynes Park, Hitching, Hertfordshire SG5 1EH.

Scottish Netball Association, Kelvin Hall, Argyle Street, Glasgow G3 8AW.
Welsh Netball Association, 82 Cathedral Road, Cardiff, South Glamorgan CF1 9LN.

Orienteering
British Orienteering Federation, Riversdale, Dale Road North, Darley Dale, Matlock, Derbyshire DE4 2HX.

Scottish Orienteering Association, 7 Lawson Avenue, Banchory AB3 3TW.

Welsh Orienteering Association, 56 Hillrise Park, Clydach, Swansea, West Glamorgan SA6 5DA.

Rounders
National Rounders Association, c/o 3 Denehurst Avenue, Nottingham NG8 5DA.

Swimming
Amateur Swimming Association, Harold Fern House, Derby Square, Loughborough LE11 0AL.

Scottish Amateur Swimming Association, Holmhills Farm, Greenlees Road, Cambuslang G72 8DT.

The Welsh Amateur Swimming Association, Wales Empire Pool, Wood Street, Cardiff, South Glamorgan CF1 1PP.

Volleyball
English Volleyball Association, 27 South Street, West Bridgeford, Nottingham NG2 7AG.

Scottish Volleyball Association, 48 The Pleasance, Edinburgh EH8 9TJ.

Welsh Volleyball Association, 136 Bwlch Road, Fairwater, Cardiff, South Glamorgan.

PHOTOCOPIABLES

The pages in this section can be photocopied and adapted to suit your own needs and those of your class; they do not need to be declared in respect of any photocopying licence.

A number of these photocopiable page relate to specific activities or suggestions in the main body of the book and the appropriate activity and page reference are given above the relevent sheet.

The swimming certificates can be presented to children when they have successfully completed each stage of the swimming programme. The mini-olympics record sheets and certificates can be used in conjunction with a school sports day or when staging your own class mini-olympics. They can be used to record all sorts of throwing, jumping and running achievements.

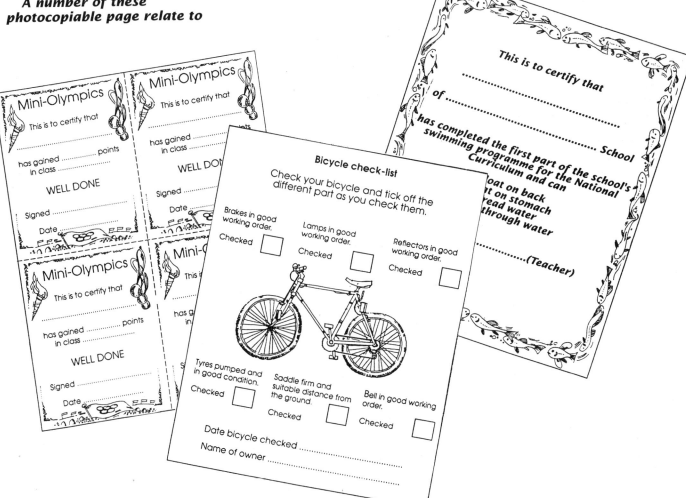

Sketch your classroom here.

Draw these items on your map.

Number of desks _____

Number of tables _____

Number of chairs _____

Number of doors _____

Number of windows _____

Number of blackboards _____

Number of cupboards _____

Number of bookshelves _____

Any other items _____ _____

_____ _____

Use this outline to sketch in the route from your school to places of interest. When you get back to school, use this outline to help you prepare a proper sketch map of the route.

Church

Police station

Fire station

School

Supermarket

Park

My house

Which of these traffic signs have you seen near your school?

Where have you seen this sign?

....

What does it mean?

....

....

Where have you seen this sign?

....

What does it mean?

....

....

Where have you seen this sign?

....

What does it mean?

....

....

Where have you seen this sign?

....

What does it mean?

....

....

Where have you seen this sign?

....

What does it mean?

....

....

Where have you seen this sign?

....

What does it mean?

....

....

Bicycle check-list

Check your bicycle and tick off the different part as you check them.

Brakes in good
working order.

Checked ☐

Lamps in good
working order.

Checked ☐

Reflectors in good
working order.

Checked ☐

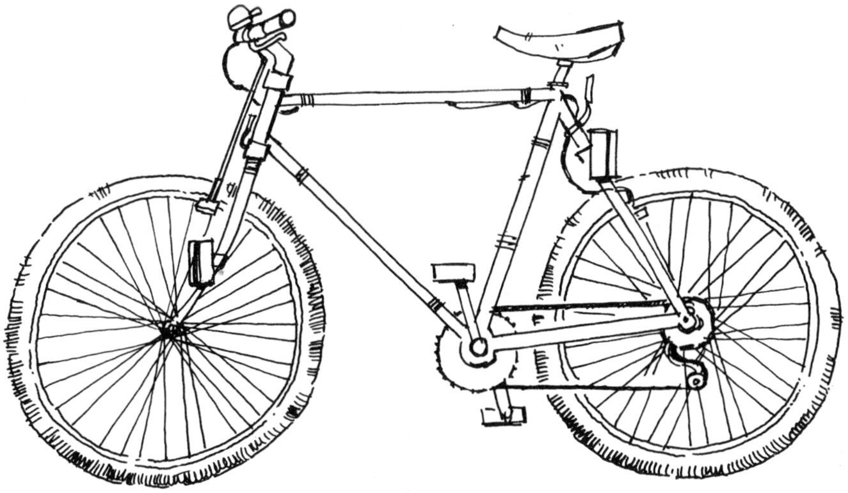

Tyres pumped and
in good condition.

Checked ☐

Saddle firm and
suitable distance from
the ground.

Checked ☐

Bell in good working
order.

Checked ☐

Date bicycle checked ....

Name of owner ....

School orienteering course

Follow this route:

Start   _ _ _ _ _ _ _ _ _ _

Check point 1   _ _ _ _ _ _ _ _

Check point 2   _ _ _ _ _ _ _ _ _

Check point 3   _ _ _ _ _ _ _

Destination   _ _ _ _ _

_ _ _ _ _ _ _ _ _ _ _ _

Clues

....

....

....

....

....

....

Swimming certificate

This is to certify that

....

of .... School

has completed the first part of the school's swimming programme for the National Curriculum and can

Float on back
Float on stomach
Tread water
Glide through water

Signed ....(Teacher)

This is to certify that

....

of .... School

has completed the second part of the school's swimming programme for the National Curriculum and can swim one width

**Front crawl
Breast-stroke
Backstroke**

Signed ....(Teacher)

This is to certify that

....

of .... **School**

has completed the third and final part of the school's swimming programme for the National Curriculum and can swim 25 metres

Front crawl
Breast-stroke
Backstroke

Signed ....(Teacher)

This is to certify that

....

of .... **School**

**has completed the school's swimming
survival programme
for the National Curriculum and can**

**Throw a rope accurately
Assist another child, using the basic
support grips
Help another child out of the water**

Signed .... (Teacher)

Mini-olympics

Record sheet for mini-olympics							
Name	Events					Total position	

Mini-Olympics

This is to certify that

....

has gained .... points
in class ....

WELL DONE

Signed ....

Date ....

Mini-Olympics

This is to certify that

....

has gained .... points
in class ....

WELL DONE

Signed ....

Date ....

Mini-Olympics

This is to certify that

....

has gained .... points
in class ....

WELL DONE

Signed ....

Date ....

Mini-Olympics

This is to certify that

....

has gained .... points
in class ....

WELL DONE

Signed ....

Date ....

Mini-olympics individual record cards

Name:

	Events							
ATTEMPTS 1								
ATTEMPTS 2								
ATTEMPTS 3								
Best score								
Total points		Well done						
Position								

Name:

	Events							
ATTEMPTS 1								
ATTEMPTS 2								
ATTEMPTS 3								
Best score								
Total points		Well done						
Position								

Name:

	Events							
ATTEMPTS 1								
ATTEMPTS 2								
ATTEMPTS 3								
Best score								
Total points		Well done						
Position								

Programme planner for class ....

Main activities

Autumn term

Spring term

Summer term